THE 1

KANT'

THE DEVELOPMENT
OF KANT'S VIEW
OF ETHICS

KEITH WARD

OXFORD
BASIL BLACKWELL
1972

THE DEVELOPMENT OF
KANT'S VIEW OF ETHICS

THE DEVELOPMENT
OF KANT'S VIEW
OF ETHICS

KEITH WARD

OXFORD
BASIL BLACKWELL
1972

ISBN 978 1 119 60431 0

Printed and bound by
CPI Group (UK) Ltd, Croydon, CR0 4YY

THE DEVELOPMENT OF
KANT'S VIEW OF ETHICS

THE DEVELOPMENT
OF KANT'S VIEW
OF ETHICS

KEITH WARD

OXFORD
BASIL BLACKWELL
1972

Edition History
Blackwell Publishing Ltd (hardback, 1972)

ISBN 978 1 119 60431 0

Printed and bound by
Lightning Source, Inc.

PREFACE

This is not a general introduction to Kant's ethics; it is not primarily concerned with expounding the *Groundwork*, the Analytic of the *Critique of Practical Reason* or the *Metaphysic of Morals*; excellent commentaries now exist on all those central ethical works. I have written for the reader or student who has some knowledge of Kant's ethical doctrine, as it can be found in one or more of the texts mentioned, but who has not the time to read all those other works in Kant's voluminous output which are relevant to and often of great importance for his view of ethics. My aim is to put the well-known doctrines in the overall context of Kant's developing philosophy. And I am concerned, not so much with the ethical doctrines themselves, as with Kant's view of the nature of morality—what he took morality to be—as it developed throughout his life. If to put something in context is to understand it better, then such a programme will help in attaining a general view of Kant's concerns in ethics; and it may well hold some surprises for those whose Kantian diet has been confined, say, to the *Groundwork*.

I think it is true to say that general verdicts on Kant's ethics are still common which such a fuller view shows to be quite inaccurate—for instance, that he was not concerned with ends of action, or that the postulates of practical reason are irrelevant additions to his central doctrines, or that he is the stern prophet of 'duty for duty's sake', without regard to considerations of human fulfilment or happiness. Such mistaken views are less common in Britain now than they used to be; but there is still widespread lack of knowledge of many of Kant's writings which are important for his ethical views, such as the *Dreams of a Spirit-Seer* and the essays on history. This book deals with most of Kant's published writings, in so far as they are relevant to ethics, and so it provides a general view of the origins, development and metaphysical context of his ethical theory.

It is probable that many readers will wish to study what I have to say on specific topics in Kant, without having to consider material which is of secondary importance for their purposes. Consequently, I have divided the text into numbered sections with appropriate headings, and have included an analytical table of contents in which the various main topics are listed.

Finally, it should be noted that I have consistently used the word 'metaphysics' in a non-Kantian sense—i.e. to mean, not *a priori* elements of knowledge, but a general speculative account of the nature of reality, derived from whatever source. I have found it convenient to use the word in this sense; and, as long as it is remembered that it is a non-Kantian sense, it should cause no confusion.

I should like to thank the editor of the *Philosophical Quarterly* for permission to use material from 'Kant's Teleological Ethics' (1971). I am also grateful to Leslie Stevenson and those who read the manuscript for my publishers, who made very helpful comments.

LIST OF TEXTUAL REFERENCES

To avoid frequent use of footnotes, I have put all references to Kant's works in the text. I have first put the page number of the English translation, where there is one; followed by the page number of the German text, thus:

(o, 61; Ber. 2, 218.)

Almost all references to the German text are to the edition issued by the Royal Prussian Academy, now the German Academy of Sciences, in Berlin (published from 1902 onwards). This is abbreviated as 'Ber.', followed by the volume and page number. An exception is *Eine Vorlesung Kant's uber Ethik*, ed. Menzer (Pan Verlag Rolf Heise, Berlin, 1924), which is abbreviated as 'Vor.'

In quoting from the *Critique of Pure Reason*, I have followed the traditional practice of citing page numbers from both the 1781 ('A') edition and the 1787 ('B') edition, thus:

(A. 561; B. 589.)

The abbreviations for the English translations I have used are listed below, in order of their appearance in the text:

ND: *Nova Dilucidatio*, 1755 (*Principiorum Primorum Cognitionis Metaphysicae*), trans. F. E. England, in *Kant's Conception of God*, pp. 211–52 (Allen and Unwin, London, 1929).

TH: *Theory of the Heavens* (General History of Nature and Theory of the Heavens), trans. W. D. Hastie, in *Kant's Cosmogony* (Maclehose, Glasgow, 1900).

R: *Kant, A Study* (selected translations), G. Rabel (Oxford University Press, 1963).

ID: *Inaugural Dissertation* (On the Form and Principles of the Sensible and Intelligible World) in SPW (below).

O: *Observations on the Feeling of the Beautiful and the Sublime*, trans. J. T. Goldthwait (University of California Press, Berkeley, 1960).

MM: 'The Doctrine of Virtue' (Part 2 of the *Metaphysic of Morals*), trans. Mary Gregor (Harper Torchbooks, New York, 1964).

PE: *Prize Essay* ('Enquiry Concerning the Clarity of the Principles of Natural Theology and Ethics') in SPW (below).

S: *Kant's Pre-Critical Ethics*, P. A. Schilpp (Northwestern University Press, Evanston, 1960).

D: *Dreams of a Spirit-Seer*, trans. E. F. Goerwitz, ed. F. Sewall (Swann Sonnenschein, London, 1900).

LE: *Lectures on Ethics*, trans. Louis Infield (Harper Torchbooks, New York, 1963).

SPW: *Kant: Selected Pre-Critical Writings*, trans. G. B. Kerferd and D. E. Walford (Manchester University Press, 1968).

KPC: *Kant: Philosophical Correspondence*, 1759–99, trans. A. Zweig (University of Chicago Press, 1967).

A and B: The first and second editions of the *Critique of Pure Reason*, trans. Norman Kemp Smith (Macmillan, London, 1933).

P: *Prolegomena*, trans. P. G. Lucas (Manchester University Press, 1953)

CPR: *Critique of Practical Reason*, trans. L. W. Beck (Bobbs-Merrill, New York, 1956).

CTJ: *Critique of Teleological Judgment*, trans. J. C. Meredith, (Oxford University Press, 1952).

G: *Fundamental Principles of the Metaphysic of Ethics*, (*Groundwork*), trans. T. K. Abbott (Longmans, London, 1959).

MEJ: 'The Metaphysical Elements of Justice' (Part 1 of the *Metaphysic of Morals*), trans. W. Hastie, in *Kant's Philosophy of Law* (T. and T. Clark, Edinburgh, 1887).

CAJ: *Critique of Aesthetic Judgment*, trans. J. C. Meredith (Oxford University Press, 1952).

OH: *On History*, trans. L. W. Beck, R. E. Anchor and E. L. Fackenheim (Bobbs-Merrill, New York, 1963).

Rel.:   *Religion Within the Limits of Reason Alone*, trans. T. M. Greene and H. H. Hudson (Harper Torchbooks, New York, 1960).

ANALYTICAL TABLE OF CONTENTS

CHAPTER ONE

THE RATIONALIST BACKGROUND

I.I INTRODUCTION

The aim of this book is to provide an exposition of the relation between Kant's ethical and metaphysical views, with special reference to works other than the first two *Critiques* and the *Groundwork*. In particular, I hope to show that, though Kant certainly did stress, as no one had previously, the categorical nature of moral obligation, yet Kantian ethics is, in a fundamental sense, a teleological ethic, concerned above all with ends of action, human fulfilment and happiness. Thus it is essentially bound up with metaphysical doctrines of human nature and destiny and cannot be adequately understood in isolation from them.

The study of Kant has always constituted a major part of philosophy courses in British Universities; and in recent years a number of new critical commentaries have added to the already impressive list of British and American Kant studies. Almost all of these commentaries, however, have confined themselves to an exposition of the *Critique of Pure Reason*; and then have often been chiefly concerned with the 'Transcendental Logic'. In ethics discussion has centred almost entirely on the *Groundwork to the Metaphysic of· Morals* and, sometimes, the *Critique of Practical Reason*. The so-called pre-Critical works—those written before the first *Critique*, in 1781—and the later works—*Religion Within the Limits of Reason Alone*, the Essays and even the *Metaphysic of Morals* itself—have been almost totally neglected.

Some of this neglected ground has been covered in *Kant's Philosophy of Religion,* by C. J. Webb, and in Mary Gregor's commentary on the *Metaphysic of Morals*. But all that exists to date on Kant's pre-Critical ethics is Paul Schilpp's work of that title—which is, as I shall indicate, rather idiosyncratic in its interpretation—and parts of Teale's book on *Kantian Ethics*.

This, however, is primarily an attempt to construct an original moral thesis on Kantian foundations, rather than an historical account of Kant's thought. There is no work in English which attempts to trace the overall development of Kant's ethical views, in relation to his metaphysical doctrines.

The consequence of this restricted treatment of Kant is that many philosophy graduates are left with the impression that Kant's chief aim was to outlaw all forms of speculative, transcendent metaphysics and to construct a purely descriptive account of the way in which we talk about the ordinary world—namely, as a world of causally interacting substances in one space and time. In ethics he is thought to have attempted, perhaps rather grotesquely, to establish that the fundamental principle of morality is the criterion of 'universalisability'—namely, that a principle is a moral principle if and only if one is prepared to apply it impartially to all agents in sufficiently similar circumstances.

These two aspects of Kant's thought—the descriptive analyses of fact-stating language and moral language—are rarely brought into an integral relation to each other. Further, the whole pre-Critical background to Kant's thinking; the problems which drove him towards a 'Critical philosophy'; the doctrine of Idealism, albeit 'Transcendental'; the 'moral proofs' of God in the two later *Critiques*; the underlying teleological view of nature; and the full working-out of a moral theology towards the end of his life—all these remain unknown to or unconsidered by a great number of those who successfully complete university courses on Kant.

I believe these less explored parts of Kant's philosophy to be of major interest in themselves, raising, as they do, the difficult and important problem of the relation between ethical and metaphysical beliefs, which was one of Kant's central concerns. They are also an essential foundation of any interpretation of Kant which seeks an accurate historical perspective. I have therefore tried to outline the development of Kant's metaphysical and ethical views in a way which may illuminate some of his better-known doctrines by tracing their origin and setting them in the wider context of his thought.

Such criticisms as I have made have been almost entirely internal ones, arising out of conflicts or obscurities in Kant's own texts. Although I think that Kant's work is relevant to much contemporary discussion in ethics (particularly, perhaps, to discussion of the relation between moral obligation and human flourishing), I have thought it better to let such relevancies occur to the reader, who will bring his own background and interests to the texts. So I have not tried to defend some form of the Kantian theory I describe. I have outlined part of a positive view of ethics which has some Kantian affinities, though also many disaffinities, in *Ethics and Christianity* (Allen and Unwin, London, 1970). I have here simply tried to present an adequate account of the development of Kant's view of ethics, throughout a period of almost fifty years, from the writing of the *Nova Dilucidatio* and the anonymous publication of the *Theory of the Heavens*, in 1755, to the remnants collected in the *Opus Postumum*, written between 1800–1803. As well as illustrating the great range of his thought, I hope the exposition will reveal the continuing centrality for Kant's ethics of certain metaphysical or religious concerns and a continuous development in his treatment of them.

1.2 EARLY INFLUENCES

A vital key to the understanding of Kant's views is the fact that his parents were both devout members of the Pietist Church.[1] Like many evangelical Christian organisations, Pietism emphasised the doctrine of justification by faith alone and the necessity of 'rebirth' as a dramatic and personal experience of conversion and salvation. It stressed the value of Bible study and corporate prayer, made no distinction between clergy and laity, and demanded the cultivation of an intense devotional life, to be outwardly manifested in charitable works. Whatever the possible dangers of such a religion, it evidently found in Kant's parents, who were materially poor, an embodiment the memory of which always continued to impress him. Thus he had set before him, from his earliest years, an example of simple piety at its best; and his deepest religious convictions never moved far from this ideal of the religious life.

However, in his early school education he also saw this type of

[1] Accounts of Kant's early life and education can be found in: F. W. Schubert, in vol. 11 of Rosenkranz and Schubert's edition of the *Sammtliche Werke* (Leipzig, 1842). One of the fullest biographies in English is: J. H. W. Stuckenberg, *Life of Immanuel Kant* (Macmillan, London, 1882), which gives a list of primary sources.

Protestantism at its worst—where the outward show of extreme
piety was valued above an undemonstrative sincerity; where
moral worth was almost replaced by emotional intensity; where
pupils were reminded constantly of their sins; and where atten-
dance at long and no doubt dreary devotional sessions was obligatory. It is not hard to see, in this rigorous training, the cause of
Kant's subsequent distaste for all forms of outward or communal
expression of belief, all emotional expressions of faith and all
ecclesiastical functions. His frequent castigation of love as a
'pathological feeling', entirely unconnected with moral worth—
which contrasts so completely with the normal Christian profes-
sion—can possibly be seen as a reaction to those often hypocritical
displays of religious emotion encouraged in his school days.

Besides Pietism, the other main influence on Kant's thought
was the philosophical rationalism which derived from Leibniz,
as systematised and elaborated by Christian Wolff. This was
taught to Kant at the University of Konigsberg by Knutzen,
a teacher he greatly esteemed. Knutzen himself managed to combine Pietism and rationalism; and the combination of simple faith
and rigorous intellect is very characteristic of his greatest pupil.

It is plain that the combination of these two schools of thought
is not easily achievable. There is the difference of an era between
the man of faith, who lives by Divine revelation and self-abnega-
tion; and the man of the Enlightenment, for whom reason is the
final judge in all matters, even those of religion, and who accepts
only what he can see to be deducible from self-evident truths.
There is no better expression of this tension of attitudes than the
Critical philosophy itself, which asserts, at one and the same
time, both the humility of reason—in its limitation to a world of
appearance—and the absolute authority of reason—in its presentation of the categorically binding moral imperative.

Kant's pre-critical writings, however, show that the influence
of Wolffian rationalism was uppermost, and indeed almost un-
challenged in his thinking for many years. This is particularly
clear in the work which he wrote in 1755, the *Nova Dilucidatio*
('A New Exposition of the First Principles of Metaphysical
Knowledge'). It is worth giving a brief sketch of this little-known
work, as it presents very clearly the rationalist doctrine of God
and nature which formed the starting-point of Kant's thinking
in metaphysics, and fundamentally influenced his view of the

nature of ethics. It may, I think, be claimed that without some knowledge of this rationalist background, the later development of Kant's view of ethics must be largely unintelligible, since that background set his problems and defined his aims in philosophy.

1.3 THE PRINCIPLE OF SUFFICIENT REASON

Kant's attitude in the *Dilucidatio* is entirely Wolffian; for though he quarrels with Wolff on some points, these are all matters of technical detail, which do not affect the general position. The world is considered to be a perfectly rational whole, the structure of which can be discovered by the human intellect, working in accordance with a few *a priori* principles—principles which are prior to, and not derived from experience. Ultimately, the logical key to the rational structure of the world is taken to be the subject-predicate proposition. All meaningful propositions assert that some subject has (or, according to Wolff, is identical with) a certain set of predicates; and any possible world can be completely described by a set of such propositions. The principle of sufficient reason (which Kant prefers to call the principle of determining reason) determines which states actually exist in this world. For it determines, for every particular thing, the set of predicates which hold of it, and it does this by excluding from it every other predicate from the sum total of possible predicates—including, of course, the negations of those predicates which do hold. There is thus a sufficient reason for every thing being as it is; and this reason operates through natural causality, whereby each state of affairs is brought into being by another state, its cause.

However, everything cannot be determined by something other than itself, for in that case there would be no truly sufficient reason for anything. Consequently, there must exist a determiner of all things which is not itself determined by anything else. If nothing determines the nature of this 'first cause', it must by the simple fact of its existence determine itself to be what it is and exclude all other possible predicates from itself—including, again, the negation of all the predicates which constitute it. But anything which, by its mere existence, excludes the possibility of its negation must be a necessarily existing being. The non-existence of such a being is absolutely impossible. Thus the first cause must be a necessary being.

B

Kant now argues that one can only conceive a being to be necessary in its existence if its nonexistence removes any possibility of conception (if it is unthinkable). This is only possible if the necessary being is in some sense itself the ground of all possibilities. For then, if it did not exist, no possibilities would remain at all. Since one can only conceive what is possible, the nonexistence of a necessary being is strictly inconceivable. So the first cause, which necessarily exists, is also the unitary ground of all possibilities. 'Whatever there is of reality in every possible notion must exist necessarily' in one unlimited being. (ND, 224; Ber. 1, 395.) This being, God, contains all possibilities in a supereminent way, and all contingent realities must be thought of as participations in and limitations of his all-reality. God must, moreover, be purely actual, eternal and immutable; for all change implies transition from potentiality to actuality, and God must be the totally actual ground which is prior to all possibility whatsoever.

Finally, Kant claims to have provided a proof of the principle of sufficient reason itself. For, as he claims to have shown, if anything exists which is not subject to that principle, then its existence must be absolutely necessary. But a necessary being must also contain in itself the ground of all possibility, and there can be only one such ground, by definition. Therefore the plurality of finite things must be completely determined by the principle of sufficient reason.

The unsatisfactoriness of these proofs need not be laboured; in the *Critique of Pure Reason* Kant examines them in detail and rejects them as founded on insupportable presuppositions. In particular, in the *Dilucidatio*, Kant assumes that there must be a reason why everything is determined to be just what it is, even if this reason in the ultimate analysis is that things must necessarily be so. But that is just what needs to be proved. The importance of this paper is that it clearly demonstrates that Kant's first philosophical interest was to defend and amplify the structure of Wolffian rationalism, and it introduces the dominant Kantian notions of 'necessity', 'totality' and 'causality' in their original, if to us unfamiliar, dress.

On the view Kant presents, there is a totality of all possible predicates. Out of this totality, the principle of determining reason determines one set of predicates in a subject, with the exclusion of all other predicates, and thus provides a reason for the being of every finite, contingent thing. The chain of reasons, which is also the chain of efficient causes, extends back to the first state of the world. Given the actual contingent existence of a first state of the world, all its subsequent states follow necessarily, according to the principle of determining reason; but the positing of that first state itself was an act of free choice on the part of God.

The act of creation, however, is not free, in the sense that it is quite arbitrary; such a view would reduce the origin of the world to blind chance. There is, it seems, a sufficient reason in God which determines that just this first state of the world should come into being and no other. And that is simply that this is the best of all possible worlds. As Kant remarks in his little paper *On Optimism*, there is only one possible world which is worthy of being created by God, since it is the best of all possible worlds, and so God must create it. His act is nonetheless free, because it is determined by motives of perfect intelligence which incline the will, and not by a mere blind power of nature.

Kant maintains that the perfect intelligence of God can, in one intuitive act, bring before his mind all possible combinations of identity and incompatibility of subjects and predicates. (Cf. ND, 219; Ber. 1, 391.) God can envisage all possibilities because his own being is the ground of them all, though in him they are unlimited by any determining principle of exclusion or logical principle of contradiction. God knows his own essence completely; and he knows with absolute certainty what contingent worlds he could bring into being, by limiting his own all-reality by the principles of identity and determining reason.

According to his perfect intelligence, then, he knows all possible worlds that could be brought into being. According to his perfect morality, his will inclines towards the best of these possible worlds; that is, the world which results in 'the greatest perfection of created things, and the greatest happiness of the spiritual world'. (ND, 237; Ber. 1, 404.) And according to his perfect power, he brings that world into being which the motives of his perfect intelligence and morality have determined. Thus the first state of the world 'directly exhibits God as Creator', for it is determined by motives of perfect intelligence and will, and it finds its sufficient or determining reason in that limiting exclusion of opposing predicates which actualises the most perfect compossible sequence of events. (ND, 229; Ber. 1, 399.) Thereafter it is senseless to ask why God should himself exist, because his non-existence is *ex hypothesi* inconceivable. There is no reason for the existence of God: 'Whatever is said to exist absolutely necessarily, exists not on account of a certain reason, but because the opposite is plainly not thinkable.' (ND, 223; Ber. 1, 394).

In the *Dilucidatio*, then, God is conceived as necessary, all-real, pure actuality, single, simple, infinite, eternal, immutable and a spirit possessed of will and understanding. In general outline, though not in detail, this series of arguments from the rational structure of the world to the existence of a necessary ground of all possibilities provides a close parallel to the 'Five Ways' of Thomas Aquinas. The basic postulate of such arguments is, as Garrigou-Lagrange has expressed it, that the greater cannot come from the less. There is no possibility without some actual existent in which it is grounded; for the notion of a merely possible entity is nonsensical. There must therefore be an actual ground of possibilities; a ground which, moreover, determines the existence of all actualities without itself being determined, even by itself. This being is consequently necessary, in the sense that, if anything is possible, this being must be actual; thus its opposite, which would be a possibility not grounded in any actuality, is impossible and strictly inconceivable.

By the same general principle, it is impossible that some quality should emerge, in time, as an unforeseen occurrence. For such an occurrence would be unintelligible, in the sense that it would not be sufficiently determined; it would have the character of a fortuitous event; and if such events could occur, there would no longer be any guarantee of the intelligibility of the world. Thus all occurrences in the history of the Universe must be sufficiently determined, and the determiner must be in some way like, but greater than, the determined effect. For there must be a similarity between the cause and its effect, if the former is to be capable of bringing into being the latter out of nothing. The perfections of all realities must therefore be contained in God, but in an unlimited way.

I.4 FREEDOM AND NECESSITY

One consequence of this view, which Kant accepts, is that every event in the history of the world necessarily follows from its antecedent determining causes; and the whole world follows necessarily from the perfect intelligence and will of God. This must be so, as long as one speaks of causes as sufficient reasons for the existence of their effects. Thus it seems that, if the world is to be fully intelligible, it must be wholly necessary—the existence and nature of God being absolutely necessary, and the existence of the world being a necessary consequence of God's existence. Is it possible, on such a view, to speak of God or man as 'free' in any sense?

Kant's view in the *Dilucidatio* is that it is possible; but it requires a definition of 'freedom', not as an entirely undetermined action—which would be merely arbitrary and therefore unworthy of an intelligent being—but as an action determined by internal motives of spontaneous inclination and intelligence. On this view, freedom is internal determination.

It is useless, according to Kant, to claim that free acts of will are entirely undetermined. That is both logically impossible, since no contingent reality is exempt from the principle of determining reason; and also unworthy of a rational being, since it would make his acts quite arbitrary. All that we mean, then, in saying that an action is free is that it is not determined externally, against one's inclinations and by the blind power of nature. It is determined, but it is determined, at least in part, by the 'acquiescence of the will in an object in proportion to the ground of an inducement by which it inclines the will'; i.e. by the will's desire for specific ends. (ND, 232; Ber. 1, 401.) 'To act freely is to act in conformity with one's impulse.' (ND, 235; Ber. 1, 403.) So we can act freely even when we are necessarily determined, if only the act we do is in accordance with our desires, so that we do not say we are compelled to do it against our will.

This view does seem to accord with many ordinary uses of the word 'free'. We say we are not free when some external compulsion is evident to us; and often that we are free if only we are able to do what we want. But one must ask whether this view of freedom is compatible with the ascription of moral praise and blame, reward and punishment. Is one justified in blaming a man for what he was determined, from the beginning of the world, to do?

Kant certainly holds, both that a man is totally determined in all his acts—necessarily so, by the principle of determining reason—and that he is morally blameworthy, and God is just to punish him for his sins. At this stage he is by no means clear in his solution of this antinomy of morality. But it is interesting to see it arise in his first work; and one strand of his proposed solution was to remain in his mature thought.

He suggests that among the complete grounds determining a particular act is the voluntary direction of actions upon either the good or the bad. Kant is here asking for a change in the point of view from which we judge the moral worth of actions. If we look at an action from the point of view of a finite observer then it does seem as though a particular immoral act is necessarily determined by previous acts and events, and ultimately by the first state of the world, directly created by God. Then it seems that God, if anyone, is truly responsible for that evil act. But Kant asks us to change our point of view and consider the whole determined course of the world as it might appear to the intuitive intellect of God. From this point of view, he suggests, one might find that among the reasons which determine that the first state of the world should be what it in fact is, are the spontaneous inclinations of human wills towards immoral ends, the voluntary decisions of human beings themselves.

As he puts it, 'The future is determined by such reasons as that amongst them the voluntary direction of actions upon what is base is the central fact. '(ND, 236; Ber. 1, 404.) The world would not have been determined in this way by God if he had not taken into account all the possible voluntary acts of men. Men choose, completely voluntarily, to acquiesce in the inclination of their wills, either towards good or bad ends; and in arranging the necessary sequence of determining reasons, God is influenced by these foreseen choices. Thus it is that acts can be completely free and yet completely determined.

Here is a clear, if embryonic, foreshadowing of the Critical reconciliation of freedom and necessity by means of the postulate of a timeless noumenal human choice, which is then expressed in the determined nexus of the spatio-temporal world. It would be too much to say that Kant clearly saw, in 1755, the doctrine that later enabled him decisively to reject an account of freedom as 'inner determination'; but the outline of his mature solution is clear enough.

1.5 THE BEST OF ALL POSSIBLE WORLDS

A second problem which arises out of Kant's account of God as creator is closely bound up with the problem of freedom, and it is the problem of evil. If all events in the world are necessarily determined, even from the first act of creation, how can one account for all the physical evils in the world? How can God be called good, and this the best of all possible worlds?

Kant's suggestion is that God wants to allow no aspect of goodness, even of a minor grade, to remain unmanifested. The whole Universe 'differentiates the manifestation of the divine glory in its infinite variety', and God will allow evils to be if some new kind of good can be elicited from them. (ND, 237; Ber. 1, 404.) Thus out of the suffering of the human race there is a certain specific good attained which could only come in that way, so that all the evils which we see are necessary means to a final end of perfect goodness.

As a whole the world is the best possible one, completely adapted to the ends of its creator. All natural occurrences are inevitable consequences of a system in which the simplest mechanical laws are so devised as to bring about the greatest diversity of effects. Thus infinite nature is an adequate expression of the infinity and glory of God. But it is necessary, in such a system, that its finite parts should obey the most general laws, and, if they are conscious, suffer and die when they conflict with the wider order. Man, as a minute function in the world-machine, is no more than a moment in the eternal development of the Universe. His sufferings only seem to be of consequence to him because he considers that nature should serve his ends; whereas the true situation is that he, as a natural being, only exists to serve the ends of nature, which are incomprehensibly great. Nature, seen as a whole, Kant writes, 'will show on all sides utter security, complete adaptation'; for the purpose of creation is the perfection of the whole, not the transitory well-being of its minuter parts. (TH, 156; Ber. 1, 322.)

In a scientific treatise on *The Causes of Earthquakes* (1756), Kant devotes a section to explaining their usefulness; and he tries to show the necessity of their occurrence to the existence of a completely harmonious whole. The terrible ravages that nature occasionally inflicts upon men are ways of testifying to its sublimity and infinity, and a 'humiliating reminder that man never can be anything more than a man'. (R, 30; Ber. 1, 472.) Thus even tragic occurrences increase one's awe at nature's immensity, and one's humility at realising one's own destiny, as 'born in order to die'.

Natural calamities have another function, too, according to Kant. That is to remind one that 'Man is not born to erect eternal dwelling-places in this theatre of vanity; his whole life has a far nobler end, and earthly goods cannot . . . satisfy our urge for happiness.' (R, 29; Ber. 1, 460.) The amorality of nature leads man to a recognition of his own moral worth and destiny. It leads him to reflect that all his earthly property must one day be relinquished; that he is always a stranger upon earth. It teaches him not to look for his ultimate end among the things of Nature; but to look beyond to its source, with which, by his moral strivings, he may claim a higher kinship.

For man does not exist only as a being of nature; he belongs also to a higher order, the realm of spirit. Thus, while the immensity of nature and its overall harmony compel man's astonishment and awe, its ruthless amorality leads him to recognise his higher destiny, by virtue of the moral law which he feels within himself. Natural calamities lead him to seek the source of his being beyond the mechanical laws of nature. As Kant writes in the rather mannered conventional style of the times to Frau von Funk on the death of her son, in 1760, 'The tender melancholy of a noble heart pondering on how worthless is most of what we think so great and important, would hold more happiness than the boisterous merry-making and loud laughter of the fools.' (R, 43; Ber. 2, 39).

Man is placed in a position wherein it is possible for him either to seek his happiness in the things of this world, or to use the world as a preparation for his proper destiny in the realm of the spirit. But the very limitations of this world lead one almost inevitably to look beyond it. Suffering brings home to man his own inadequacy and the unconcern of nature with his helplessness; and the tragedy of death reinforces a sense of the worthlessness of a purely natural life.

Though Kant thus attributes to nature a general moral and purposive order, he regards it as 'criminal folly' to speak of particular interventions of God in the natural order; and so, for instance, to treat the unfortunate victims of natural disasters as targets of God's vengeance. To do that is to imagine that nature serves our convenience, and to interpret the Divine intentions according to our own lights. These things happen to just and unjust alike; and, as he points out, 'The Christian Peru is tossed about just as was the heathen one.' (R, 29; Ber. 1, 460.) It is plain, then, that nature does not serve the moral ends of man; nor is man the end of nature, for which it exists. It is 'the totality of nature [which] is a worthy object of God's wisdom, and we are part of it' (R, 29; Ber. 1, 460); 'The whole is the best, and everything exists for the sake of the whole.' (*Reflections on Optimism*; R, 42; Ber. 2, 35.)

There is an internal conflict present in this view, which was to remain throughout all Kant's work. On the one hand, Kant's rationalism leads him to stress the perfection of the whole universe, and to see each individual part as a relatively unimportant though necessary feature of a grand design which, taken as a whole, is the most coherent, economical and comprehensive possible. On the other hand, his Pietistic background leads him to see each human being as having an infinite spiritual destiny, and a unique and incommensurable importance in his own right. It is not easy to see how man can both be a minute part in a perfect but impersonal natural order, and also have a personal worth which is greater than that of nature. Of course, Kant holds that man's destiny extends beyond nature to an infinite spiritual life. But then why should he ever be part of nature, and so subject to its ills and vicissitudes? And what part does the physical universe play in the development of the uniquely valuable human individual?

It is probably true to say that this problem was never adequately resolved by Kant, though it occurs frequently throughout his life. In his last writings he returns to it, and proposes a fuller explanation of the relation of nature and humanity (cf. chs. 8.3 and 4); but in his earliest works he seems content to reiterate the rationalist theory that each individual is a necessary part of the most perfect possible whole. Kant's developed theory of ethics appears in its proper perspective only when it is seen as springing from, reacting against, but never completely abandoning, this view of the world propounded by Leibniz and Wolff, for which the best of all possible worlds is completely and necessarily determined by the intelligence of an infinite and perfect God.

In the context of such a view, the ethical life is most naturally seen as a contemplative one. One acts in accordance with one's knowledge. So to act well it is necessary to know reality in its true perfection. The highest goal for man is primarily contemplative knowledge of the perfection of the whole, and only secondarily action in accordance with such knowledge. The will does not have a predominant role to play in the rationalist view of ethics. It is probably fair to see Kant's later doctrine of *practical* reason as a reaction against such a high evaluation of the intellect and of pure contemplation. But the reaction is essentially one which remains within the ambit of rationalism, and can be understood only in the light of its characteristic concerns with the coherence, unity, universality and necessity which make the moral realm itself amenable to the demands of reason. It is therefore important to see the form of speculative rationalism from which Kant began, before tracing the development of his ethical views towards the anti-speculative but still rationalistic theory which characterises the Critical view.

1.6 GOD AND NATURE

The young Kant was not just an abstract metaphysician. He was a promising scientist with at least two important findings to his credit—the nebular hypothesis, later credited to Laplace, and the observation of the influence of the moon on the tides, with a consequent retardation in the earth's rotation.[2] His rationalist metaphysics was combined with an acceptance of Newtonian mechanics, in the formulation of a theory of general cosmic evolution, which he published anonymously as the *General History of Nature and Theory of the Heavens*, in 1755.

In this work he explicitly sets himself to derive the nature and motions of the heavenly bodies from a primitive state of the world by wholly mechanical principles, even castigating Newton for postulating a direct intervention of God in maintaining the solar system in motion, instead of seeking a mechanical derivation for that also. Accepting the general principles which Newton had worked out to apply to the solar system, Kant generalised them to cover the whole universe, and elaborated a theory of

[2] Cf. the excellent discussion in the Translator's Introduction to *Kant's Cosmogony*, by W. D. Hastie (Maclehose, Glasgow, 1900).

cosmic evolution which did not require God's intervention to explain it at any point. Yet he held that such a programme was in no way opposed to belief in God. On the contrary, Kant states that as he began to elaborate this scheme, he 'saw the glory of the Supreme Being break forth with the brightest splendour'. (TH, 18; Ber. 1, 222.) For it is precisely in the perfect order and rich diversity of the ends produced by the simplest mechanical principles that the existence of a supremely wise creator is established. The more one discovers the simplicity of the basic laws of nature, and their adequacy for so many wonderful and beautiful purposes, the more 'the mind is seized by a kind of rapture when it considers how such magnificence and greatness can flow from a single law, with an eternal and perfect order'. (TH, 135; Ber. 1, 306.)

Leibniz had written that an omniscient God would create a world in which 'there is obtained as great variety as possible, along with the greatest possible order'. (*The Monadology*, trans. R. Latta, Oxford University Press, 1898; p. 249.) Thus the ordered simplicity of the basic laws of Newtonian mechanics, which give rise to all the diversity and richness of the visible universe, is the most powerful testimony to the existence of God that there could be. 'There is a God for this very reason that even in a chaos nature cannot proceed in any other than an orderly and regular way.' (TH, 26; Ber. 1, 228.)

Kant's argument to the existence of God, as expressed in the essay on 'Living Forces' and later developed in the *Inaugural Dissertation*, is that the world is a totality of substances, standing in relations of mutual interaction. But real relations cannot be understood through the mere existence of substances, he holds, because each substance is complete in itself. Therefore 'Something else is required in addition whereby their mutual relations may be grasped by the intellect.' (ID, 75; Ber. 2, 407.) This 'something else' must be a common unitary cause which relates substances in one world-whole, and it must be a necessary being which does not itself stand in relations of interaction with finite substances, but which externally establishes the interaction and harmony of all substances which depend upon it. Thus substances cannot truly interact unless they have a common cause and a harmonious dependence upon it. In this way, the mere fact of genuine relationship proves the existence of a God, as the common cause of all substances and the one who establishes the necessary harmony according to which all things interact. The further fact that the intelligible relationships of substances are the simplest possible consistent with the greatest possible variety of phenomena enables one to attribute intelligence and power to this unitary ground of nature.

The laws of nature are expressions of the inner forces, inherent in substances, by means of which they 'seek to unite themselves'. These laws are to be discovered, not merely by inspection of sensible phenomena, but by metaphysical investigation of the intelligible relations of substances, which alone can reveal the origin and cause of things, 'the universal bond by which all substances and their states belong to the same whole which is called a world' and which provides the reason for their being thus and not otherwise. (ID, 62; Ber. 2, 398.) The search for such intelligible laws of connection is therefore guided by the concept of a supreme God, who develops the complicated and harmonious structure of natural laws from chaos, without any arbitrary intervention. So for Kant, far from there being any incompatibility between science and theistic belief, scientific enquiry is made possible by the notion of a rational God who will order the world according to general intelligible laws. And it is itself a means of revealing the wisdom and glory of God as expressed in the works of nature.

Kant thus takes a form of the teleological argument for God's existence very seriously. In fact he asserts that 'whoever does not obstinately resist all conviction must be won by these irrefutable reasons'. (TH, 19; Ber. 1, 222.) But he decisively rejects any form of the argument which concludes from the existence of particular occurrences to the direct intervention of God. He denies, for instance, that one must infer a Divine intervention at the birth of each animal or human person. Organisms must obey natural laws of reproduction, and appeals to 'inner forms' or 'organic elements' fail to explain anything. It is only from the adaptation of the world as a whole to ends that one can infer to a unitary ground with will and understanding. Indeed, it is more sublime and shows greater Divine wisdom to say that a human being comes into existence according to the ordinary operation of natural laws, than to say that God has to keep interfering in the mechanism to produce souls at the appropriate time.

In the *Beweisgrund*, Kant rejects the idea of supernatural intervention on four counts. First, it implies that God is not wise or powerful enough to construct laws which do not stand in need of constant intervention. Second, it fails to provide the possibility of a philosophical proof of the Christian doctrine of creation *ex nihilo*, since it implies that matter is, in Aristotelian fashion, regarded as a distinct substance upon which final laws must be imposed. Third, it leads to inevitable and damaging conflict with natural scientists, who can always produce a naturalistic explanation of any alleged activity of nature according to ends and thus overthrow any apologetic which is based on an appeal to supernatural explanations. And fourth, it actually serves as a barrier to the progress of science, in causing one to stop the search for natural explanations for every event.

In place of such arguments for special Divine intervention, Kant directs our attention to the whole panoply of nature in its most general conditions, and suggests that it shows an inner purposiveness, not imposed arbitrarily by outside interventions. 'If such conditions [of harmony and lawfulness] pervade all nature', he writes, 'there must be in the essence of things a tendency to unity and coherence which points at one unique great cause.' (R, 54; Ber. 2, 96 f.) Again, he asserts, 'We do not say, God is the ground for the inner possibility of things by His Will. We say infinite Nature, the essence of all things, renders the highest desire of God fertile of consequences.' (R, 54; Ber. 2, 91.) This statement seems to mean that we are not to picture God as a person making arbitrary acts of will which bring the universe into being and adjust it from time to time. But we are to regard God as *himself* the ground of the inner possibility of all things. Being is such that it allows the final ends envisaged by supreme wisdom to come about by a natural and necessary process of development.

Kant adds one final qualification to this remarkably modern view of the teleology of nature, and that is to say that the teleological argument cannot prove the existence of the all-perfect being of traditional theology (which he thinks he has proved by his special form of ontological argument). For though 'the things of the world do give evidence of an intelligent author of great wisdom, power and goodness, [we cannot infer] that it is omniscient, omnipotent and the most perfect of all beings'. (R, 58; Ber. 2,

160.) We must assert that there is a unitary ground of being (a
'community of cause') to account for real relationships between
substances; and we must attribute intelligence and understanding
to the ground of being to account for the inherent finality of
natural laws. But we cannot infer the exact degree of this Divine
wisdom from its natural effects in the world.

1.7 THE ROMANTIC VISION OF NATURE

In Kant's earliest works one can discern the eclectic spirit which
makes his philosophy so complex and rewarding, by its fusion of
different strands of thought. The rationalism of Leibniz and
Wolff is combined with the scientific mechanics of Newton. To
these is added a comprehensive vision of nature as a developing,
evolving process. Pietism enters, with its stress on the unique
importance of the individual soul, with ultimate moral freedom
and an eternal destiny. And the whole is crowned with a Romantic
view of nature as not just a mass of particles in motion, but a
symbol for a spiritual reality which is its real ground.

This Romantic doctrine, to be developed in the *Critique of
Judgment*, is clearly adumbrated in the *Theory of the Heavens*.
Kant writes, 'In the general silence of nature and the calm of the
senses, the hidden intuitive power of the immortal spirit speaks
an ineffable language and presents us with undeveloped ideas
which can be sensed but not described.' (R, 26; Ber. 1, 367.) And
again, in the *Beweisgrund*, 'A well-disposed soul may obtain
moral certainty as he quietly contemplates the beauty and order
of nature.' (R, 56; Ber. 2, 116.) The sublimity of nature is something that fills the soul with rapture and elevates it to a contemplative level of pure and disinterested delight. Thus Kant
encourages one to contemplate nature, until certain feelings are
aroused, which have an obscure but nonetheless cognitive
content. When one contemplates the infinity and majesty of
nature, the rich and orderly diversity brought about by the
simplest mechanical laws; when one views the transitoriness of
all finite things, and the sublime indifference of nature to birth
and death alike, one may find oneself possessed by feelings of the
utmost rapture and wonder. As Kant writes, in a passage which
deserves quotation in full,

When we follow this Phoenix of Nature, which burns itself only in order to revive again in restored youth from its ashes, through all the infinity of times and spaces . . . in order to fill eternity as well as all the regions of space with her wonders, then the spirit . . . sinks into profound astonishment. But unsatisfied even yet with this immense object, whose transitoriness cannot adequately satisfy the soul, the mind wishes to obtain a closer knowledge of that being whose Intelligence and Greatness is the source of all . . . and with what reverence must not the soul regard even its own being, [which] . . . is destined to survive all these transformations. (TH, 154 f; Ber. 1, 321.)

Here, in a passage which contains many presages of his future doctrines, Kant urges one to see at the same time the infinity of nature and the transitoriness of all her works. And he finds in man's soul a dignity which surpasses all the works of nature, evoking a feeling of reverence, in the recognition of man's kinship with the Primary Source of the whole universe, which one can thus contemplate with a detached and complacent gaze. Further, he finds in the spectacle of cosmic evolution and continuous creation the analogy of a spiritual life that 'may go on to fill all the infinitude of time and space with stages of perfection in thought that grow on to infinity, and which has to approach, as it were step by step, the goal of the supreme excellence of the Deity, without, however, being ever able to reach it'. (TH, 167; Ber. 1, 331.) Thus the immortal soul will soar above all that is finite and be able to view all nature in its harmony and perfection. The contemplation of nature in her infinity and transitoriness raises the soul to a sense of its own sublimity and eternal destiny, which affords 'a sort of delight which only noble and pure souls can feel'. (R, 26; Ber. 1, 367.)

Two major elements of Kant's later thought are clearly set out here. First, the goal of the complete reduction of natural explanation to purely mechanical laws. And second, the search for a 'moral proof' of the existence of God, which has to be based somehow upon a recognition of nature's inability to account for the existence of moral ends, and of the kinship of the soul with that perfect reason which is itself the source of nature. In this early essay, Kant has not yet hit upon the idea of 'freedom' as providing the necessary starting place for such a proof, and he seems only to talk of a 'hidden intuitive power of the Spirit'. He could never be content with such an appeal to intuition; but

he was to have a long struggle before he found a rational basis
for this intuitive conception of a spiritual world of beings, ever
evolving to fuller perfection, and united in a spiritual community
under one all-perfect Reason. Nevertheless the sources of Kant's
developed moral theory are to be found in these pre-Critical views
on the spiritual constitution of the universe; views for which he
continually sought some means of rational justification.

There is, however, a continual tension in Kant's thought,
which becomes most evident in the *Dreams* of 1766. But it is
already present in the *Theory of the Heavens*. For he writes

> I am not so devoted to the consequences of my theory that I should
> not be ready to acknowledge that [it] cannot entirely escape the reproach
> of its being undemonstrable. Nevertheless, I expect from those who are
> capable of estimating degrees of probability that such a chart of the
> infinite, comprehending, as it does, a subject which seems to be destined
> to be for ever concealed from human understanding, will not on that
> account be at once regarded as a chimera, especially when recourse is
> had to analogy. (TH, 146 f.; Ber. 1, 315.)

Analogy, rationality, economy and probability are stated to be
the methods of constructing Kant's theory. But he admits that
these matters may be not only strictly undemonstrable, but
even beyond the range of human understanding altogether.
Scepticism here vies with metaphysical theory. And, contrasting
the confident assertions of some paragraphs with the sceptical
hesitations of others, I think it is plain that Kant was driven both
by a desire to believe in his spiritual vision and by the equally
strong awareness that he could not justify it.

His early writings on the subject of nature, then, foreshadow
the developments which were to lead to his moral proof of God;
but it is clear that he had not yet managed to fit his early intuitive
vision into a rationally systematised whole. This vision of nature
as an awe-inspiring product of a supreme intelligence, as something which, though in itself an amoral system, is yet the sphere
of spiritual evolution in which mankind must struggle to win a
higher spiritual destiny through transcending the nature which
bore him, is the basic vision which underlies and makes possible
Kant's subsequent view of ethics. Its sources are clearly set out
in the deeply Romantic and yet rationalistic writings which
constitute Kant's earliest published works.

CHAPTER TWO

THE DOCTRINE OF MORAL FEELING

2.1 THE BASIS OF MORALITY IN FEELING

The earliest work in which Kant deals specifically with moral questions is the *Observations on the Feeling of the Beautiful and the Sublime*, written in 1763. Morality is not, of course, the main subject of this work, which is expressly concerned with aesthetic emotions. It seems fair to suppose, then, that one will not find in it a complete or adequate outline of Kant's moral beliefs. But it does contain many interesting and important observations on ethics.

Kant begins by distinguishing the feelings of the beautiful and the sublime as 'finer feelings', which one can enjoy longer than other feelings without satiation and exhaustion; and which 'presuppose a sensitivity in the soul, so to speak, which makes the soul fitted for virtuous impulses'. (O, 46; Ber. 2, 208.) Kant holds that 'among moral attributes true virtue alone is sublime'. (O, 57; Ber. 2, 215.) There are also many good moral qualities which cannot be identified with 'true virtue', and these are characterised as 'amiable, beautiful and noble'. Kant thus makes a clear distinction between 'moral qualities' and 'the virtuous disposition'. There are many moral qualities which are valued in men. But the question of virtue, of the moral worth of the person as an agent, is quite a different question from that of whether or not he possesses these moral qualities. Thus Kant instances 'compassion'—sympathetic concern for others—and 'complaisance'—the desire to please—as moral qualities, but maintains that the possession of them bears no relation to the moral worth of the agent. For of themselves they may be used for immoral ends, as when sympathy for one individual blinds one to a greater but more remote duty, or when complaisance leads one to adopt immoral ways for fear of giving offence.

Further, Kant is already clear that action in accordance with

c

virtue is not at all the same as action *from* virtue, i.e. action which
is performed because it is right. Only the latter has true moral
worth. So in the *Observations* he clearly sets out the central
Critical doctrine that the moral worth of the agent lies only in
acting from virtue.

When he comes to say what 'acting from virtue' is, however,
he suggests 'universal affection toward the human species', as
opposed to particular affections for particular objects. (O, 58;
Ber. 2, 216.) And this he calls a 'principle . . . to which you
always subordinate your actions', as opposed to a sentiment which
you just happen to feel on occasion. He seems to be characterising
the maxim of virtue as a feeling, though of a generalised, or
universalised, kind. As such, it is, he says, 'colder' than more
particular feelings, i.e. less intense. We may indeed cultivate 'the
universal love of man', but it can hardly be an intense emotion;
it must be a more dispassionate sentiment. Nevertheless, it is
characterised by Kant as a 'feeling' of peculiar generality, which
does not spring from speculative reason. 'These principles [of
virtue] are not speculative rules, but the consciousness of a feeling
that lives in every human breast . . . I believe that I sum it all
up when I say that it is the *feeling of the beauty and the dignity of
human nature.*' (Kant's italics; O, 60; Ber. 2, 217.)

These features of beauty and dignity are central to Kant's
approach to ethics. Beauty is associated with the love of one's
fellow-men and the attraction one may feel for others. Dignity is
associated with the respect for the sublimity of human nature,
both in oneself and in others, which derives from man's transcendence of empirical nature, and which finds expression in
respect for others and a sense of personal honour and worth.
Beauty and dignity; love and respect; attraction and repulsion,
are always the two poles between which moral feeling oscillates.
In the *Dreams*, Kant speaks of love and respect as forces of
attraction and repulsion which govern the relations of beings in
the spiritual world (cf. p. 37 f.). And in the *Metaphysic of Morals*
he repeats the same idea on three occasions: 'All the moral
relations of rational beings, which comprise a principle of harmony among their wills, can be traced back to *love* and *respect*';
'The principle of love commands friends to come together, the
principle of respect requires them to keep each other at a proper
distance'; 'When we are speaking of laws of duty . . . we are

considering a moral [intelligible] world where, by analogy with the physical world, *attraction* and *repulsion* bind together rational beings [on earth].' (MM, 163; Ber. 6, 488. MM, 141; Ber. 6, 470. MM, 116; Ber. 6, 449.) So it seems that Kant did not change his early view that morality was intimately associated with the feeling of the beauty and dignity of human nature.

Far from conforming to the popular caricature of a pedantic and rationalistic scholar who had little appreciation of the human sentiments, Kant always asserted that morality is closely bound up with a certain complex feeling for human nature. The problem with which he wrestled for many years was that of the nature of the relation between the 'feeling' and the ground or motivation of moral action. His Critical doctrine, of course, was that the moral feelings—which he cites as the feeling of pleasure in doing one's duty and susceptibility to be moved by practical reason; the pain of conscience in violating duty; benevolent affection and reverence for law—'lie at the basis of morality, as *subjective* conditions of our receptiveness to the concept of duty'. (MM, 59; Ber. 6, 399.) But they are not 'objective conditions of morality'. It is by virtue of having the disposition to such feelings that a man is subject to obligation. But 'moral feeling . . . yields no knowledge . . . we no more have a special *sense* for the [morally] good and evil than for *truth*'. (MM, 60; Ber. 6, 400.) Feeling is simply the subjective receptiveness in the mind to the action of practical reason; and though it 'makes us aware of the necessitation present in the concept of duty', consciousness of such feelings must follow, and cannot precede, the consciousness of the moral law, as it affects the mind. (MM, 59; Ber. 6, 399.) Without the susceptibility to such feelings no man could be under obligation; but the actual occurrence of the feelings 'can only follow from the thought of the law'. Practical reason determines the moral feelings to arise in us; all we contribute is the susceptibility for such feelings, and some ability to cultivate them by contemplating the moral law itself. The feelings, once present, may give rise to moral actions; but they must be caused by practical reason, and cannot by themselves alone be the basis of moral obligations.

In 1763, however, Kant had not developed his notion of a reason which was essentially practical, and it appears that he then regarded feeling itself as the ground or incentive of virtuous

action. He says, speaking of the ways in which moral motives
are supplemented by non-moral motives which accomplish the
same ends, 'Since even this moral sympathy is not yet enough
to stimulate inert human nature . . . Providence has placed within
us still another feeling that . . . can set us in motion'. (O, 61;
Ber. 2, 218.) It sounds as if feeling, specifically the feeling of
'moral sympathy', is here accepted as the ground of morality,
which may be supplemented by *other* feelings to move us to
moral action. And, though it is true that Kant goes on to distinguish 'principles' from 'impulses', and to affirm that the truly
virtuous man must act from universal principles, nevertheless
he seems to mean by 'principle' simply a certain unchangeability
of feeling—'the noble ground remains and is not so much subject
to the inconstancy of external things'. (O, 65; Ber. 2, 221.) Thus
the moral feeling is characterised by its 'unchangeability' and
'universality of application'.

The Kant sees that it is characteristic of virtue that its principles
must be universal; that it is a matter of principle rather than of
emotion; and that it is bound up with a 'universal affection' and
'esteem' for persons, or human nature. But he fails to explain
that difference between the 'universal moral feeling' and other
feelings which lies in the fact that, whereas the occurrence of
feelings depends upon our sensible constitution, for which we
are not responsible, the 'love of man' is an absolute obligation
for all men. It is not enough to say, as he does, that the feeling
'lives in every human breast'. For that would still be a contingent
matter of fact. It would not, at least on his subsequent understanding of 'obligation', account for the obligation to have that
feeling.

The Critical doctrine was to allocate this feeling to the
causality of reason in its practical use, and in that way deliver it
from the subjectivism which Kant attributes to all feelings. This
will account for the fact that acting from virtue is acting on a
principle, not just on the basis of a feeling—a fact for which
Kant is unable to account adequately as long as all rational
principles are attributed to speculative reason alone. In the
Observations, however, Kant still seems to be committed to an
account of morality in terms of feelings, and so he is unable to
adhere consistently to the principle he formulates in the *Prize
Essay*, written in the same year: 'All the actions prescribed by

ethics . . . cannot be called obligations, so long as they are not subordinated to a single end, necessary in itself.' (PE, 32; Ber. 2, 298.) For when moral principles are interpreted simply as relatively universal, unchanging, feelings, they must ultimately share with all other human feelings a dependence upon the contingent psychological dispositions of men; they cannot enjoin an end, necessary in itself.

Kant does not shrink from accepting this conclusion. In fact in some remarkable passages he appears to suggest that only a few men are able to act on moral principles. Indeed, he even says, 'I hardly believe that the fair sex is capable of principles.' (O, 81; Ber. 2, 232.) Moreover, he asserts, it is positively a good thing that this is the case! He writes, 'Among men there are but few who behave according to *principles*—which is extremely good'; for there is nothing worse than a resolute man who sincerely acts on mistaken principles. (O, 74; Ber. 2, 227.) The virtuous man is just one among others—he is the melancholy man—in the varied pattern of human life. And, as a human character-type he easily becomes, Kant points out, a man of self-will—'earnestness inclines toward dejection, devotion toward fanaticism, love of freedom to enthusiasm . . . he is then much to be feared'. (O, 66; Ber. 2, 221 f.) Even acting from principles—the good will itself—may be dangerous if it is founded on a 'perversity of feeling and the lack of an enlightened reason'. (O, 66; Ber. 2, 222.) The strong will to do what is right may degenerate into a wilful obstinacy and intolerance of others. Kant was no stranger to the doctrine that the man of principle and high virtue may well be morally objectionable.

So the purposes of nature require that, as well as men of principle, 'there exist those who act out of good-hearted impulses'; those who base all their acts on self-interest and those who always act out of regard for their own honour. All this is for the best, concludes Kant, for 'the different groups unite into a picture of splendid expression, where amidst great multiplicity unity shines forth, and the whole of moral nature exhibits beauty and dignity'. (O, 75; Ber. 2, 227.) The underlying conception here is the Leibnizian doctrine that this is the best of all possible worlds, so that it expresses, through parts which often seem grotesque when taken in isolation, one grand design, which 'presents the great portrait of the whole of human nature in a stirring form', and constitutes a 'noble whole'. (O, 73; Ber. 2, 226.)

This metaphysical view, combined with Kant's great personal interest in anthropology—an interest evidenced by his frequent papers on anthropological subjects, and by the fact that he lectured on anthropology every year throughout his University career (cf. *Anthropology*, 1798, in Ber. 7)—led him to see the extraordinary diversity of human feelings and attitudes as parts of one sublime design in which all these diverse parts contribute to the most perfect possible organic whole. Morality, with the feelings on which it is founded, is just part of this rich and varied pattern of motives, which expresses the intelligible relations of spiritual substances. On the other hand, it is difficult to see just how moral judgments can fit into such a scheme, in which everything must be just in order as it is, so that there can be no place for the notions of moral freedom and absolute obligation which were Kant's heritage from Pietism.

Thus there is again a tension in Kant's ethical thinking between the interpretation of morality in terms of feeling and its inter-pretation in terms of necessary obligation and freedom. But though this tension is undeniably present, Kant's earliest remarks on ethical theory show that at this stage he followed the British moralists (especially Hutcheson) in founding morality on feeling.[1] He concludes the *Observations* with an exhortation that he would hardly have expressed so unguardedly after the formu-lation of his Critical theory, with its clear distinction between reason and feeling in ethics; namely, that one should seek to 'elevate the moral feeling in the breast of every young world citizen to a lively sensitivity'. (O, 116; Ber. 2, 256.)

2.2 THE FORMAL PRINCIPLES OF MORALITY

The influence of the British moralists is even clearer in the *Prize Essay* of 1764 (written in the previous year), where Kant writes, 'Only in our times has it begun to be realised that the

[1] Kant was certainly acquainted with the work of Hutcheson, Shaftes-bury and Hume. They are referred to in correspondence, and in the 1765 *Nachricht* (S, 8; Ber. 2, 311)—cf. p. 33. Hutcheson's doctrine of moral feeling is specifically referred to, with approval, as providing 'a beginning to fine observations', in PE, 34; Ber. 2, 300.

faculty of representing what is *true* is *knowledge*; whereas the faculty of perceiving what is *good*, is *feeling*.' (PE, 33; Ber. 2, 299.) We *perceive* the true (that which is the case, independently of us) and express our knowledge in 'indivisible concepts'. But we *sense* the good (which is only found in things as related to feeling creatures, not in things themselves) and we do so by means of an 'irreducible feeling'. As we know the true by means of concepts, so we sense the good by means of one distinctive and irreducible feeling. One could, like Hutcheson, speak of a 'moral sense' or feeling which acquaints one with the good, but one must note Kant's comment that the good is found only in relation to feeling creatures, so it is not, presumably a property of things themselves.

Moreover, he says, 'The judgment, 'this is good', is completely unprovable and is an immediate effect of the consciousness of the feeling of desire combined with the representation of the object.' (PE, 33; Ber. 2, 299.) He seems to state in this passage that one perceives an object; and if the perception is accompanied by a conscious feeling of desire (the 'feeling for the good' mentioned above) one immediately says, 'this is good'. This corroborates the view that moral judgments do not express cognitions (or even sensings) of objective properties, but are immediate effects of quite subjective feeling-reactions to the ordinary properties of objects. The occurrence of the feeling is naturally 'completely unprovable'; i.e. it is a brute fact of our constitutions, as feeling creatures.

Kant also writes, 'If an action is immediately represented as good . . . the necessity of this action is an unprovable material principle of obligation.' (PE, 33; Ber. 2, 299.) He thus derives the concept of obligation from sensations of goodness, in such a way that acts sensed as good become necessary ends of one's own action, unprovable obligations. So far, Kant may seem to agree with the British moralists exactly. Nevertheless, he is here adding something, and something distinctively rationalistic, to this account of morality in terms of moral feeling. And that is the exposition of a formal element in morality, a primary formal principle of moral judgment.

It had been the doctrine of the *Dilucidatio* that the principles of non-contradiction and sufficient reason could together provide all possible knowledge of the world. But as Kant became clearer on the distinction between real and logical relations, he came to admit the necessity of 'unprovable' material grounds of knowledge in addition to the formal principles of knowledge. That is, he came to admit a sheer empirical 'givenness' which could not be reduced to analytic statements of identity of subject and predicate or simply deduced from the reality of God by the principle of sufficient reason.

In the *Prize Essay* Kant explicitly limits the task of philosophy, however provisionally, to the analytic one of exhibiting, in Newtonian fashion, the basic elements of experience. Thus he holds that philosophy cannot begin, like mathematics, from clear, simple definitions and proceed by synthetic deduction— for example, beginning from the concept of 'substance' and thereby deducing the nature of the world from the definition. Rather, philosophy must begin from experience, analyse it and aim at definitions only as the end result of such analysis. There is a plurality of diverse 'elementary concepts', which are the subjects of material unprovable judgments, and which it is the task of philosophy to discover and enumerate, but which philosophy cannot further explain or 'prove' by deduction from higher principles.

It is clear that, under the influence of Newton and the inductive procedures of physical science, Kant has moved away from fully-fledged Wolffian rationalism; away from a synthetic mathematico-deductive method in philosophy towards an analytic and empirical method. But he retains the fundamental principles of reason as formal principles which necessarily govern the organisation of knowledge; and so he still resists a Humean sort of empiricism. It is also noteworthy that he writes of this 'analytic method' as a provisional one. He holds open the future possibility of a final synthesis of human knowledge under necessary principles, even though such a synthesis must wait for the analytic method to be fully explored first. So an *a priori* universal science remains the Kantian ideal, which he was never entirely to abandon.

But it must be put into at least temporary abeisance; so that in the *Prize Essay*, the presence of the word 'unprovable' with reference to material principles is to be taken as signifying a decisive break with pure rationalism and a limitation of the rational to one, formal, aspect of knowledge. Kant says, 'Nothing flowed from the first formal principle of our judgment of the true, where no material first grounds are given' (PE, 32; Ber. 2, 299); but, conversely, without formal principles the material grounds could yield no concepts, and thus no knowledge. So also in morality, Kant holds, there is no content to morality without material grounds (which he finds in 'moral feeling'); but such feelings could not give rise to knowledge of obligation, or moral judgment, without certain formal principles.

These principles Kant cites as twofold: first, 'Do the most perfect deed that you can'; and second, 'Omit that whereby you hinder the greatest possible perfection.' (*loc. cit.*) Presumably the situation is that the material element of morality is a certain feeling which arises when one perceives specific objects and is a given datum of human experience. This gives some content to the otherwise empty concept of 'perfection'. But it is the formal principle that one should do whatever thus falls under the concept of perfection, or omit things that hinder the implementation of such acts, which makes feelings into distinctively moral feelings, and gives rise to the concept of 'ends necessary in themselves', which forms the basis of morality.

By drawing attention to these formal elements of morality Kant may indeed be said to be supplementing and completing the doctrine of the British 'moral sense' school, as he claims (cf. *Announcement of Lectures, 1765–6*, S, 8; Ber. 2, 311); for the addition of his formal principles does allow an entrance for the concept of 'obligation' which presented such a great difficulty for the British moralists and for moral sense theorists in general. The difficulty is that if 'goodness' is simply a property which is sensed, or ascribed because of the occurrence of a specific feeling, it becomes hard to see how ascriptions of 'goodness' can give rise to absolute obligations. The occurrence of feelings can move one to action; but, since all feelings are contingent, they cannot give rise to obligations, or specifically moral (i.e. absolutely necessary) prescriptions. The formal principle which Kant offers as a supplement to a moral sense theory is intended to bridge this gap between feeling, action and obligation, by laying down the general rule that one ought to do whatever acts are felt to have the property of 'goodness'. But the whole material content of morality—the belief that specific things and acts are good —must, he believes, derive from feeling.

2.3 THE DEVELOPMENT OF THE CRITICAL THEORY

Kant concludes the *Prize Essay* by noting that 'the supreme, fundamental concepts of obligation must . . . be more surely determined'. (PE, 34; Ber. 2,300.) He is not satisfied that he has reached certainty with regard to the primary foundations of morality. Indeed he says, 'It has still to be discovered . . . whether the faculty of knowledge or feeling . . . exclusively decides the primary principles of practical philosophy.' (*loc. cit.*) The 'primary principles' in question are probably the 'unprovable material principles', since he usually refers to the formal principles as 'rules', in the *Prize Essay*. And the important phrase in this passage is 'exclusively decides'. For it shows Kant already to be asking the question which is of decisive significance for his ethical theory, 'Given that our primary unprovable obligations have both a form and a matter, are they determined, *qua* obligations, by the matter (feeling), so that the form simply connects the feelings with action? Or are they determined by the formal element so that no feeling can give rise to obligations unless it falls under necessary formal requirements?'

There is not much doubt that the *Prize Essay* strongly inclines to the former answer; partly because of the emptiness of the formal rules which Kant is at this stage able to supply; partly because of his use of the terminology of Hutcheson with regard to moral feeling; and partly because of the fact that he could not yet see how a purely rational principle could be an effective motive to action, or the ground of moral feeling.

Yet the latter answer is the explicit and undoubted answer of the *Groundwork*; and thus it is significant that the question should have been raised by Kant at least as early as 1764. It seems probable that Kant, as a rationalist by training, would desire to see morality as determined purely by rational principles. Yet such a procedure would require a synthetic, deductive methodology, deriving all specific obligations from some *a priori* supreme principle. And that methodological ideal had been renounced in the *Prize Essay*.

The ideal was to recede even further and reach its point of greatest attenuation in the *Dreams of a Spirit-Seer*, the most sceptical yet tortured of Kant's works. But then it was to make a marked recovery in the 1770 *Inaugural Dissertation*, and finally settle down into a sort of *via media* position with the *Critique of Pure Reason*. So Kant's early development may be divided into four main periods—the early rationalistic period of the *Dilucidatio*; then an increasingly sceptical period, culminating in the *Dreams* of 1766; after that, a brief return to a strongly rationalist position, in the *Inaugural Dissertation*; and finally the development of the Critical view that principles of reason are formal, regulative and heuristic, and have the function of making scientific and moral knowledge possible. His view of ethics naturally parallels this course of development, and the *Prize Essay*, written in 1764, at the beginning of the sceptical period, shows the increasing ascendancy of Newtonian, analytic methods in philosophy.

This inductive method left him with many unprovable material principles of ethics, given by moral sense or feeling. And he was content to point out that there was also a formal element in morality which remedied some of the deficiencies of ethical systems based solely on moral sense or feeling. But he also expressed, in the last paragraph of the *Essay*, what seems to be the tentative hope of a future synthetic method which might demonstrate the superiority of form over matter, reason over feeling, as the determinative though not the sole element in the construction of moral principles.

My conclusion, then, is that the *Prize Essay* exhibits in its ethical views the same espousal of a Newtonian method of analysis and rejection (perhaps temporary, Kant suggests) of a Leibnizian method of synthetic deduction from clear first definitions, as is evident in the metaphysical part of the work. It is in many ways a much less rationalistic work, therefore, than the ethics of the Critical period. But the solution which Kant offers to the problems of ethics is a tentative one. The compromise he attempted between Leibniz and Newton (between Wolff and the British moralists, in the context of ethics) was unstable, and Kant was not to be satisfied until he found a more rationalistic solution, which was yet fully able to take account of the empirical 'givenness' of human experience. He could not finally do that, however, until he had developed the Critical conception of reason as promulgating formal rules governing all experience.

2.4 KANT'S DISSATISFACTION WITH MORAL SENSE THEORIES

Kant's awareness of the tentative and unsatisfactory nature of his early views on ethics is expressed in some notes which are to be found pencilled into an interleaved copy of the *Observations*, and which are usually dated around 1764 or 1765.[2] Paul Menzer claims that Kant sees now, for the first time, the impossibility of founding morality on feeling. But this judgment seems unduly dogmatic. From the textual evidence, which is obscure and often contradictory, all one can say is that Kant did often evince scepticism about moral feeling. 'The universal love of humanity has something high and noble about it, but it is chimerical' (S, 68; Ber. 20, 25); 'man never participates in the happiness or unhappiness of others until he himself feels contented' (S, 68; Ber. 20, 25); 'it is very ridiculous to say: you ought to love other men: one must much rather say: you have good reason to love your neighbour' (S, 70; Ber. 20, 45); and, finally, 'the great endeavour to mitigate the evil of others is merely derived from the desire of the soul in which these feelings arise for its own approval' (S, 67; Ber. 20, 144).

From such remarks, which are almost cynical in tone, it does seem as though Kant is keenly aware of the inadequacy of the actual feelings of men to be the basis of a sound morality. Accurate descriptive accounts of human psychology tend to undermine those theories of moral sense which presuppose the possession of a fundamentally good heart. Such a thing is perhaps rarely found in the world, and the very conception of it may even be 'chimerical'. This realisation and the dissatisfaction occasioned by it are expressed in another well-known remark from the marginal notes: 'Everything goes past like a river . . . where do I find fixed points in nature, which cannot be moved by man, and where I can indicate the markers by the shore to which he ought to adhere?' (S, 73; Ber. 20, 46.)

In looking for 'fixed points' which cannot be moved by man, Kant is looking beyond the phenomena of human feelings to find a more secure basis for morality; but he has not yet developed

[2] Ber. 20, pp. 1–192. They are fully commented on in: P. Menzer, 'Der Entwicklungsang der Kantischen Ethik in den Jahren 1760–1785' (*Kant-Studien*, 1898 and 1899).

a clear alternative to 'feeling'. There is even a tension, moreover, in his notion of 'feeling'. The 'feeling of the beauty and the dignity of human nature', of which he speaks in the *Observations*, cannot easily be equated with the 'consciousness of the feeling of desire combined with the representation of the object', which he posits as moral feeling in the *Prize Essay*. So, not only is Kant unsure whether morality can be founded on feeling. He is totally unclear about what he means by 'feeling', about whether it is a mere feeling of desire or a more complex emotional response which incorporates a specific vision of the nature of human existence.

The tension and dissatisfaction which characterise Kant's thought at this time come to a head in the *Dreams*, which may be regarded as the culmination of the second phase of Kant's development, the retreat from Wolffian rationalism. But, before turning to that remarkable work, it is worth noting Kant's announcement of his lectures on ethics for 1765–6, in which he shows none of the dissatisfactions with moral sense theories which may be taken to be expressed in the 1764 fragment. In the *Lecture Announcement* he states, 'The judgment concerning moral righteousness can be easily and correctly known by the human heart through what is called sentiment.' (S, 75; Ber. 2, 311.) Though it is understandable that a University lecturer might keep his doubts to himself, this announcement does at least show that what Kant had most fully worked out at that time, and what he presumably regarded as satisfactory enough to be presented in public, was closely similar to the theories of Shaftesbury, Hutcheson and Hume (especially of Hutcheson), which, he says, 'although unfinished and deficient . . . will receive that precision and supplementation which they now lack'. (S, 8; Ber. 2, 311.) This supplementation, one may assume, was to be provided by the addition of the supreme formal principles of obligation, as they are sketched in the *Prize Essay*.

This weak conception of the 'formal' could not satisfy Kant's rationalist instincts for long. But before this conception could be strengthened, Kant had to come to terms with his reluctant attraction to Swedenborg, which was at once to plunge him into the depths of metaphysical scepticism and show him the way to establish the synthesis of the Critical philosophy and thereby escape the unpalatable consequences (for him) of moral sense theories of ethics.

CHAPTER THREE

THE DREAMS OF METAPHYSICS

3.1 THE INFLUENCE OF SWEDENBORG

In 1763,[1] Kant wrote to Fraulein von Knobloch, 'I am waiting longingly for the book which Swedenborg intends to publish' (R, 73; Ber. 10, 45); and soon afterwards he bought all six volumes of Swedenborg's *Arcana Coelesti*. That quite remarkable work, written by a highly respected Swedish nobleman who held important positions of State and made a number of significant technical discoveries, claims to be an account of his spiritual conversations with angels and inhabitants of other realms and his visits to Heaven and Hell, together with an esoteric interpretation of the hidden meaning of the Bible. Like many works of occultism, it seems to be a mixture of profound imaginative insight and preposterous nonsense. But one of the most impressive things about Swedenborg was that he did seem to possess paranormal powers of prediction and cognition—at least, there was a great deal of *prima facie* evidence of his powers, to which Kant refers in the letter just quoted. Moreover, the doctrine of a kingdom of spiritual beings which he claimed to have verified by visionary experience was remarkably similar to Kant's own speculative account of the spiritual nature and evolution of the human soul. So it was perhaps natural that Kant should have shown a marked interest in Swedenborg's findings.

Out of this interest came the strangest and most tortured of Kant's writings, the *Dreams of a Spirit-Seer*, written in 1766. Written, as he says, in response to enquiries about his opinion of Swedenborg, it seems to pour scorn upon the claims of the visionary, and, indeed, to deride any form of speculative metaphysics as on a par with the delusions of spirit-seers. Yet Kant also constructs a speculative system which is in broad agreement with Swedenborg's claims and admits that 'hope for the future'

---

[1] For a discussion of this disputed dating, cf. D, 160.

inclines him to accept such a system of universal spiritual evolution as true. Even though this may be a 'mere inaccuracy', it is, he says, one 'which I cannot easily remove and which in fact I never want to remove'. (D, 86; Ber. 2, 349 f.) And he wrote in a letter to Moses Mendelssohn, dated 8 April 1766, 'The attitude of my own mind is inconsistent . . . and I cannot help cherishing an opinion that there is some validity in these experiences.' (D, 162; Ber. 10, 69.) Visionary speculation and rational scepticism seem to be equally strong, if competing, forces in Kant's mind at this time; and this strange work expresses a very strong attraction for, and an equally strong revulsion against, the sort of spiritual vision which Swedenborg presented.

Kant begins his own metaphysical 'dream of a spiritual visionary' by remarking that the conception of 'spirit' is not a difficult one to form, since it is 'merely negative', consisting in the denial of the properties of material existence. 'The possibility of the existence of immaterial beings can be supposed without fear of its being disproved, but also without hope of proving it by reason.' (D, 46 f.; Ber. 2, 323.) There may, it is true, be some impossibility of which we are unaware, so that, strictly speaking, we are not entitled to say either that spirits are possible or that they are impossible. Yet if they remain incomprehensible, one must remember that even the possibility of the existence of material things is incomprehensible (i.e. we do not know the sufficient reason for their existence) though of course the fact of their existence is ascertained by the senses.

So one is free to form a concept of purely spiritual beings, incomprehensible though it will be. And one may further suppose that 'a spiritual essence is inmostly present in matter . . . every substance . . . must have an inner activity as the reason for its external efficiency'. (D, 53 f.; Ber. 2, 328.) Nevertheless, 'the influence of beings of incorporeal nature can only be said to exist, but it can never be shown how it proceeds, nor how far its efficiency extends'. (D, 59; Ber. 2, 331.) Though nature may ultimately be determined by spiritual forces, science cannot be concerned with them. For there are no criteria for showing how immaterial principles may interact with mechanical ones; nor for telling where they are present and where absent; nor how they make any specific differences at all to the world as we know it.

Thus any appeal to immaterial principles as an explanation of physical occurrences is a mere subterfuge; we must limit ourselves, in science, to tracing out as far as possible the mechanical laws of motion, as enumerated by Newton. Though there may well be limits to the possible progress of mechanistic science, this must not prevent the application of Newtonian principles in every sphere until those limits become apparent.

This is the force of Kant's later Critical doctrine of the constitutive nature of the principle of causality, that it is a necessary condition of having any scientific, systematic explanation of the world. In so far as scientific knowledge is to be possible, it must consider only 'those causes of the world's phenomena which rest on the laws of motion of matter alone'. (D, 59; Ber. 2, 33.) It may not give the ultimate truth about the world. Perhaps good reasons will emerge for thinking that it does not. But if that is the case such 'ultimate truth' is not the province of scientific explanation and is therefore not a proper object of scientific knowledge.

Since the empirical, material world is, as Newton demonstrated, ruled by mechanical principles, which are not spontaneously active and self-determining, and since spirits must be conceived as immaterial, purposive and self-determining, 'we should have to regard the human soul as being conjoined in its present life with two worlds at the same time . . . as a member of the spiritual world it receives and gives out the pure influences of immaterial natures . . . [thus] heaven would be properly the spirit-world, and this we would have to seek neither above nor below', for it is the spiritual reality underlying this world. (D, 60; Ber. 2, 332.) Man is a member of two worlds. In the corporeal world he is subject to mechanical principles of Newtonian physics. In the immaterial world, there is a 'communion in conformity with spiritual natures', a spiritual connexion of parts with one another, which is realised in moral action and which is not a proper subject of scientific investigation. The visionary metaphysics of a spiritual and material world united in man, which Kant here outlines, was to remain a constant and important influence on his subsequent thinking. Whatever Kant's attitude to Swedenborg's claims to occult perception, the Swedish spirit-seer had a formative part to play in the development of Kant's mature theories.

3.2 THE VISIONARY METAPHYSICS OF THE DREAMS

One of the most interesting passages of the *Dreams*, in view of the later development of Kant's thought, is one in which he attempts, from 'an actual and universally conceded observation', to establish the probability of the existence of a *'mundus intelligibilis'*. The observation in question, he says, does not precisely furnish evidence for an intelligible world; but it does give occasion for reflecting that the postulation of such a world is at least not unreasonable. The observation he has in mind is the nature of moral obligation, or, as he calls it, the 'feeling for morality'.

'The sense of morality [he writes] would be the sensation of the dependence of the individual will upon the will of all, and would be a consequence of the natural and universal interaction whereby the immaterial world attains its unity.' (D, 64; Ber. 2, 335.) The undisputed fact of the moral life is 'a certain sensation of restraint', which sometimes compels us to adapt our intention to the welfare of others. One can conceive this restraint as the activity of a foreign will in us, which subjects even our own inclinations to some sort of external consensus of opinion. This experience has a parallel in the development of rational judgment, in which we perceive the dependence of our own judgment upon the common sense of man. So there is a sort of 'unity of reason' among all thinking beings, which arises through some force which compels us to refer our own judgments to those of others, so as to render them concordant.

As in reason, so in morals, the sense of obligation and the feeling of benevolence both spring from a primary impulse to consider the will of others outside ourselves. The moral rules which govern our action, just like the rational rules which govern our thinking, are dependent upon 'the rule of the will of all', which may be conceived as a moral community of immaterial beings. There is an impulse in us which bids us consider the wills of others and bring them into conformity with our own will, so that, with other acting beings, we may form a moral community.

Now these, Kant claims, are the evident facts of moral experience. But, he asks, is it not possible to conceive these mutual relations of moral beings as the consequence of an actual

D

spiritual interaction, expressed in the spiritual forces of love and respect, just as gravitation is a consequence of the universal forces of attraction and repulsion, in the physical world? We could then explain the sense of morality as the result of a real mutual dependence of a world of spirits upon one another in a 'system of spiritual perfection', whose laws of cohesion would be just those laws of 'universal will' known intuitively by moral sense.

The influence of Rousseau as well as Swedenborg is evident in these passages. The *Social Contract* and *Emile* came to Konigsberg in 1762, and they had a marked influence on Kant for some years thereafter. This is acknowledged in the well-known note pencilled into a copy of the *Observations*: 'There was a time when I despised the masses . . . Rousseau has set me right . . . I learn to honour men.' (S, 48; Ber. 20, 44.) Kant's Pietistic upbringing makes it certain that this 'conversion' was not so sudden or unprepared as is sometimes claimed. But the influence of Rousseau on Kant's development is undeniable. And in this section of the *Dreams* he attempts a synthesis of Rousseau's obscure notion of a 'general will' which is other than a mere consensus of all individual wills, with Swedenborg's notion of the intelligible world of spirits.

'The morality of an action concerns the inner state of the spirit', Kant writes; and the consequences of such spiritual actions only become fully apparent in the 'immediate communion of spirits'. (D, 65; Ber. 2, 336.) There one's true position in the system of moral intelligences will become plain and one will find oneself already in Heaven or Hell, in accordance with the strict laws of moral justice. 'The moral quality of our actions can, according to the order of nature, never be fully worked out in the bodily life of men, but it can be so worked out in the spirit-world, according to spiritual laws.' (D, 65; Ber. 2, 336.) As Swedenborg claimed, in the realm of spirits each man is, even in this present life, in Heaven or Hell—that is, he is related to other spirits in accordance with inevitable laws of spiritual cause and effect. But this system of spiritual relationships is only imperfectly expressed in the material world, so that there is often an apparent discrepancy between moral action and its just consequences in this life. What cannot be worked out in the order of nature, with regard to man's moral development can, however, be completed in the spiritual world, and in that world the consequences of hidden purposes and motives will inevitably make themselves known, even though on earth they remain largely hidden.

So the feeling for morality is 'only a manifestation of that which actually takes place in us', the felt constraint upon our will to harmonise with the general will. (D, 64; Ber. 2, 335.) 'The phenomenon of moral impulses . . . [is] the consequence of an actual force, consisting in the fact that spiritual natures flow into each other . . . the natural and universal interaction whereby the immaterial world . . . forms itself into a system of spiritual perfection according to the laws of this sense of morality.' (D, 64; Ber. 2, 335.)

These laws Kant is able to interpret by the use of the notion of a 'general will': 'We recognise that in our most secret motives we are dependent upon the rule of the general will and thence there arises in the community of all thinking beings a moral unity and a systematic constitution according to purely spiritual laws.' (D, 64; Ber. 2, 335.) All the empirical phenomena of morality, and in particular that moral feeling which gives the distinctive sense of being morally obliged or constrained, are simply appearances of active relations between men, *qua* members of an intelligible world; and these relations are given a formal characterisation by Kant, in that they sustain a systematic harmony under the rule of the general will.

In this full-bodied dogmatic metaphysics, the general will is conceived as a really existing unitary source of all particular wills, in which these are freely incorporated. Already the *Groundwork* articulation of the formal characteristics of moral obligation as universality, respect for the ends of others, self-legislation of the law and membership of a harmonious moral community, are implicit in the *Dreams*. But they are there given as real metaphysical characteristics of the relations of beings in an intelligible world, a world which is another aspect, or the true moral ground, of the world of sensibility.

At this stage in the development of his thought there were two main problems which Kant needed to resolve. First, there was the problem, bequeathed by the moral sense theorists, of how contingently occurring human feelings could give rise to a sense of absolute and necessary obligation. Second, there was the

problem, bequeathed by rationalism, of how rational principles—
which, Kant held in the *Prize Essay*, were purely formal—could
be action-guiding, or move one to act. In the *Dreams*, he is able
to suggest a preliminary solution to both these problems, by his
appeal to the doctrine of two distinct worlds, the sensory and the
intelligible. The formal principles of reason are interpreted as
the laws of action of beings in a real intelligible world; and moral
feelings are interpreted as sensory appearances of this system of
intelligible relationships. As a sensory, feeling being, one
experiences the sense of constraint which, as a rational legislative
member of the spiritual world, one imposes upon oneself. The
Dreams therefore marks a decisive advance from the weak notion
of the 'formal' in the *Prize Essay*; from a bare, 'do the best you
can' to the fully-fledged formal principle which was to be eluci-
dated in the *Groundwork*: 'Act so as to create and sustain a
universal harmony of ends in an intelligible community of freely
legislating wills'.

3.3 THE PRIMACY OF MORALITY

This conception of a world of spiritual beings, united in one
community under an all-perfect Reason, is a clear development
of Kant's own views, as expressed in the *Theory of the Heavens*.
But, having expounded it, he now seems to disavow and reject it
completely.

Such metaphysical constructions, he says, are dreams just
as much as are any of Swedenborg's delusions. Both alike are
'secrets in the deluded brains of dreamers'. (D, 84; Ber. 2, 348.)
And he seems to make his position clear in a letter to Mendelssohn, referred to above (8 April 1766), where he writes, 'My
analogy [between moral influx and gravitational force] is not
intended seriously.' (Ber. 10, 69.) Even in the Preface to the
Dreams, he says, 'The main part he [the reader] will not understand, another part he will not believe, and the rest he will laugh
at.' (D, 39; Ber. 2, 318.) He speaks of the postulation of an
intelligible world of spirits as a 'dogmatic supposition', a 'fairy-
tale from the fool's paradise of metaphysics', 'a futile dream'. The
dreams of visionaries and of speculative metaphysicians too, he
says, are no more than mere 'farts or belches'.

In face of this rather extreme metaphysical scepticism, the

only solution he sees is to adopt the injunction of Voltaire's Candide, and 'go into the garden and work'. The cultivation of a well-disposed soul is, after all, better than attempting to penetrate into the secrets of other worlds: 'All the noisy systems of doctrine . . . can hardly decide anything about the future destiny of the righteous', and so perhaps one should not 'meddle with idle questions, but confine oneself to what is useful', namely, the pursuit of moral perfection. (D, 121; Ber. 2, 373.)

In fact, he suggests, it is not only unnecessary to base morality on speculative doctrines about the nature of the world; it would be positively wrong to do so. For speculative arguments are not logically conclusive and are always subject to doubt. Moreover, morality does not need a certain knowledge of metaphysical truths to back it up, since the moral law of itself commands categorically. Finally, if such metaphysical certainty was possible and did serve as a justification for moral action (which it is not and does not) then such a state of affairs would be positively undesirable, since all men would then act morally from prudence, not by the free decision of a will unswayed by any speculative considerations. Moral commitment should remain even when metaphysical certainty is shaken. And he suggests, foreshadowing the Critical doctrine of the postulates, that the metaphysical suppositions of God and immortality are in any case not founded upon dispassionate argument, but must be somehow based on morality itself. As he puts it, 'There probably never was a righteous soul who could endure the thought that with death everything would end.' (D, 121; Ber. 2, 373.) Though undeveloped, the hint is clear that belief in a spiritual reality may be somehow founded on the fact of moral commitment itself, rather than on speculation.

One might see the main argument of the *Dreams*, then, as being to establish the independence and logical priority of morality over theoretical speculation. Metaphysics is confined to an analytic role, resolving concepts into their fundamental elements. It cannot provide knowledge of the ultimate nature of reality. It is at most 'the science of the boundaries of human reason'. (D, 113; Ber. 2, 368.) The Wolffian ideal of a synthetic dogmatic metaphysics is now decisively rejected; and thus the *Dreams* marks the nadir of Kant's metaphysical interests.

'Now I lay aside this whole matter of spirits . . . since I have

finished and am done with it', he writes; 'in future it does not
concern me any more'. (D, 90; Ber. 2, 352.) But the fact is that it
did continue to concern him for the rest of his life. And the
visionary metaphysics of the *Dreams* which he so vehemently
disavows in the very same work is of fundamental importance
for an understanding of Kant's view of ethics.[2] Indeed, it is in
that visionary section of the *Dreams* that one can discern the
genesis of the notion of the 'formal' supreme principle of ethics
in its unmistakably Critical interpretation.

The *Dreams* is thus a significant work in the development of
Kant's ethical theory. It expresses the transition from the moral
sense theories of the British moralists to a more intellectually
based theory of ethics. It shows the origin of the formalistic
conception of the categorical imperative, and its true character
as a principle of the systematic and harmonious development of
ends, in a visionary dream of a spiritual world. It exposes the
influences of Wolff, Newton, Swedenborg and Rousseau in
forming the theory. And it lays the foundation for the doctrine
of the primacy of practical reason, in renouncing visionary
speculation, setting bounds to the scope of reason, and insisting
on a commitment to morality which is independent of any
speculative claims.

3.4 INTELLECT AND SENSIBILITY

Kant's sceptical resolution to renounce speculative theorising
about spiritual reality was extremely short-lived. Four years after
the *Dreams* was published, Kant's *Inaugural Dissertation* re-
affirmed the dogmatic rationalist view that the intellect can
obtain knowledge of an intelligible world by its own constructive
activity. Rejecting the Leibnizian notion that the phenomena of
sensibility are confused appearances of intelligible realities, Kant
supposes, instead, that the sensible world is the object of the
faculty of sensibility and the intelligible world the object of the
faculty of intellect, and that these two faculties are quite distinct.
'Sensibility[3] is the receptivity of a subject by which it is possible

---

[2] Cf. for instance, the recurrence of the analogy between gravitation and
moral relations in MM, 116; 141; 163; Ber. 6, 449; 470; 488.

[3] I have retained the word 'sensibility', rather than Kerferd's rendering
'sensuality', because it has an established place in British Kant studies.

for the subject's own representative state to be affected in a definite way by the presence of some object.' (ID, 54; Ber. 2, 392.) One can distinguish between two necessary constitutive elements of all sensory representations: 'matter' and 'form'. The matter of sensation is the actual quality of that sensation—e.g. the particular shade of red or the precise timbre of sound. The occurrence of this quality 'involves the presence of some sensible thing'. But, of course, its exact quality depends upon the nature of the subject. All sensible qualities are 'modifications of inner sense'.

The form of representations is the way in which they 'are coordinated by a certain natural law of the mind'. 'For the various things in an object which affect the sense to coalesce into some representational whole there is needed an internal principle in the mind, by which those various things may be clothed with a certain specificity in accordance with stable and innate laws.' (ID, 55; Ber. 2, 393.) The mind, working in accordance with the 'stable and innate' laws of representation relates the primitive sensa (Kant's own word) in various ways to one another. But the mental representation cannot be called an image of the object, 'for objects do not strike the senses through their form', they do not project their own form on to human sense-mechanisms. The laws of sensibility which coordinate various sensa will consequently depend upon the special nature of the knowing subject.

Intellect, on the other hand, is a faculty of spontaneity, by which through its own constructive act the intellect posits concepts of objects or relations in accordance with the laws of pure intelligence. These are not intuitions of intelligible objects, for there is no faculty of intelligible intuition. They give 'a symbolic cognition of things intellectual . . . through universal concepts in the abstract'. (ID, 60; Ber. 2, 396.) But this knowledge, even though symbolic, is knowledge of things as they really are, since the laws of intelligence are the laws which govern the structure of reality. The constructive symbolic acts of intellect give knowledge of the real intelligible world because they are limited repetitions of the Divine act of reason which brings objective reality into being.

3.5 THE MATHEMATICAL ANTINOMIES

Kant was soon to see the difficulty of supposing that, whereas the laws of sensibility are purely subjective, the concepts of intellect can be relied upon to give knowledge of reality. And so the Critical problem was to be generated: how can the objective validity of the principles of intellect be justified? (Cf. letters to Marcus Herz, especially 21 February 1772; Ber. 10, 123 ff.) But in the *Dissertation* he thought that the doctrine of the 'double derivation' of knowledge of objects from the nature of the mind was able to resolve the two antinomies of reason which he had at that time discovered.

These were the mathematical antinomies, stating, first, that space and time were infinite and that they were not; second, that space and time were infinitely divisible and that they were not. Both parts of each antinomy, Kant thought, could be apodeictically proved by reason; and this fact seemed to put reason itself in jeopardy. But though Kant had seemed to accept a radical scepticism in the *Dreams*, it did not satisfy him for long. He was a reconciler by nature, and in this eighteenth-century dispute, which was mainly between the dogmatic metaphysicians, in the tradition of Leibniz and his indivisible monads, and the inductive scientists, following Newton and his absolute, infinitely divisible space, Kant played true to form.

With the aid of the doctrine of transcendental idealism—the view that space and time are empirically real (for sensibility) but transcendentally ideal (non-existent for intellect and hence in reality)—he felt able to reconcile both views. For pure reason, which gives insight into the rational essence of things, demands and assumes limits in which it may find complete satisfaction, in the form of indivisible simples and absolute totality. These demands of reason are satisfied in the objective world of intelligible reality, since that world itself is a creation of perfect reason. But these concepts of 'the simple' and of 'an infinite whole' are not capable of being represented in sensible intuition. For the laws of representation which relate sensa are just the forms of space and time. These are necessarily subjective laws, merely methods of organising phenomena. Since they are simply ways of organising inner sense, one can neither say that in themselves they are infinite and made of infinitely divisible parts nor that they are not. Thus the demands of reason, while justified, cannot be represented in sensible intuition.

The mathematical antinomies are thus resolved by an appeal to the 'double derivation' of all knowledge of objects from the two faculties of sensibility and intellect. This doctrine also explains why noumena cannot be bound by the laws of space and time, or why 'objects do not strike the senses in virtue of their form'. (ID, 55; Ber. 2, 393.) For the form of the intelligible world, which intellect reveals, is 'the principle of possible influxes [interactions] of the substances which constitute the world', a 'principle by which it may be possible that the states of the several things whose subsistence is none the less independent each from the other should be related to one another mutually as grounded [caused] determinations'. (ID, 51 f.; Ber. 2, 390.) This intelligible form of the world is a rational objective nexus, 'the eternal principle of every contingent form'. The forms of space and time, which are the forms of sensible representation only, are certainly not rational or objective ideas, and therefore it is impossible that they should exhibit the true form of the intelligible world. This is the basis for Kant's claim, not only that one cannot tell whether the forms of space and time are forms of the real world, but that one can know that they are not.

So reason demands that one should think of the world as an absolute totality of independent but interacting simple substances, related according to necessary laws of causality. And at this stage of his thought Kant considers that these demands of reason give insight into the noumenal world. In addition they have two further functions. First, they limit merely sensible concepts to their own sphere and prevent them from making dogmatic and unjustifiable assertions about the whole of reality, which would render the concept of an intelligible world ruled by final causality absolutely impossible. And second, they issue in an Ideal of perfection, 'which is a common measure for all other things in so far as they are realities' (ID, 59; Ber. 2, 396), and which has a double aspect, according to whether we regard it from the speculative or the practical point of view.

In the speculative sense it is God, the 'principle of the coming into existence of all perfection', the necessary first cause in whom all the world finds the unity of its being and the harmony of its laws. In the practical sense it is moral perfection, which is thus

the supreme culmination and exemplar of the pure concepts of
morality, just as God is the supreme culmination and exemplar
of the pure concepts of speculative metaphysics.

3.6 INTELLECTUAL KNOWLEDGE OF MORALITY

Moral concepts are now said to be 'cognised not by experiencing
them but through the pure intellect itself'; and the first principles
of moral judgment, as of metaphysical knowledge, are known
only through the pure intellect, and must be added to experience
by the intellect. (ID, 58; Ber. 2, 395.) By analogy with the
speculative acts of intellect, they will be applied to concrete
phenomenal situations, as interpretative categories in terms of
which those situations must be understood morally. But whereas
the speculative categories are the general formal concepts under
which actually existing phenomena must be understood, the
practical judgments of intellect apply formal rules of action to
possible free acts in the world.

These purely formal principles would be followed by any
purely rational being which had no other springs of action.
Intellect naturally applies these principles to each and every
phenomenal situation, under the presupposition of the complete
freedom of the agent. Thus in every situation the free rational
agent has a pure practical understanding of what must be done
by him in that situation. Just as man must understand his
experience theoretically in terms of the pure speculative concepts;
so he must understand it practically in terms of the pure formal
principles of free action. Thus intellect legislates of itself the
essential principles both of knowing and of acting. Both these
are added to experience on the occasion of receiving sense-
impressions and they add a non-empirical determination to
human experience which cannot adequately be explained by
attempts to reduce it to purely empirical data.

It is the doctrine of the *Dissertation* that the pronouncements of
speculative reason are constitutive of the noumenal world. They
give knowledge of transcendental reality. Since practical reason
is in all respects similar to speculative reason, because they derive
from a common source in the spontaneity of the human intellect,
one may also hold that the principles of action which are promulgated by intellect actually exemplify or bring to light the

objective Moral Law which is inherent in the structure of intelligible reality. For God brought the world into being by a moral act, and the world, as the best of all possible worlds, is chosen by a supremely wise and perfectly moral intelligence. Therefore the intelligible structure of transcendental reality must be a moral structure, and the 'principle of the possible inter-actions of substances in a world', which is the form of the intelligible world, must find its consummation in the freely chosen activity of moral agencies within a harmonious whole.

Thus, as a moral being acting under the presupposition of freedom man legislates formal principles of action which exemplify the ideal principle of intelligible relationship, and which, if implemented, would bring into being the perfect moral kingdom, wherein the practical demands of intellect would be adequately met. At this stage Kant's notion of the moral law as consisting of a formal principle of action is fully developed. But this principle is still conceived as describing a real intelligible relationship in the noumenal realm of spirits.

3.7 THE COLLAPSE OF THE DISSERTATION VIEW

Despite his protestations and disclaimers, by 1770 Kant had succumbed to the dream of metaphysics. But the metaphysics of the *Dissertation* was in turn to be totally destroyed by a fatal incoherence it contained. For it is part of the doctrine that 'all the primitive affections of these concepts [of space and time] are outside the barriers of reason and so cannot be explained intellectually in any way'. (ID, 72 f.; Ber. 2, 405.) The forms of sensibility are beyond the jurisdiction of intellect; they do not conform to what the laws of intellect prescribe. Yet they alone must form the basis of nature, in so far as nature is empirically known.

There is eventually, then, an element of irreducible sheer factuality in human cognition of nature which cannot be compre-hended by means of the principle of sufficient reason. Thus there seems to be no way in which one can assert the exis-tence of simple substances acting according to the principle of sufficient reason within nature, phenomenally understood. Kant's division between the sensible and intellectual faculties is reflected in the difficulty of unifying the phenomenal and the noumenal worlds. It is clear that he wishes to state that the phenomenal world is simply the appearance or representation of the noumenal world. But his study of space and time as the forms of sensibility leads him to say that phenomenal nature is not amenable to the demands of intellect at all. The world which intellect is competent to understand with the aid only of its inborn principles cannot be more than obscurely indicated in nature. 'Perceiving' and 'knowing' are two distinct functions which cannot be united in any satisfactory way. Yet Newtonian science is surely valid precisely of the phenomenal world. It accounts for the perceived motions of the planets and the behaviour of observable bodies. And one of Kant's chief concerns was to show that the doctrines of Leibniz could form an adequate metaphysical foundation for Newtonian mechanics.

What Kant needs, therefore, is a proof that the metaphysical demands of reason can be justifiably grounded in phenomenal experience. For only in that way can they provide the desired metaphysical backing for Newtonian science.

It was primarily the discovery of the mathematical antinomies that led Kant to posit an absolute distinction between the faculties of intellect and sensibility. For they could be resolved by allowing that one set of assertions was true of the intelligible world, while the contrary set of assertions was a necessary consequence of the successive and subjective production of the coordinating laws of sensibility. But this solution leads to the unpalatable conclusion that the axiomatic principles of Newtonian science can be true only of a world which is unobservable in principle.

This position is quite untenable. If Kant was to retain the general outline of his solution to the antinomies—namely, that they were grounded in distinct faculties of knowledge—he would have to find a satisfactory way of relating both faculties to the same, presumably phenomenal, world. But if such a relationship to a common world is granted, it is plain that the precise solution which Kant gave—that both terms of the antinomies are true, of different worlds—will have to be emended.

Kant now has to say that the demands of intellect can be met in the phenomenal world, for only on that presupposition is Newtonian science possible. So the antinomies seem to reassert themselves with all their old force. If the demands of intellect can be met in the phenomenal world, it cannot be maintained that the antinomies arise because of the impossibility of giving these demands phenomenal exemplification. Thus Kant was led to make a further distinction between the non-sensible faculties of understanding (intellect) and reason.

It is the understanding which is the source of those intellectual demands which *can* be met in phenomenal experience—what Kant was to call the constitutive concepts of understanding. These are the concepts of substance, cause and necessity, which find their justification in the fact that they are necessary to the forming of scientific judgments about the world.

Kant distinguishes from these constitutive concepts those further demands of the intellect which lead to the postulates of ultimate simples and absolute totality in the world. These demands are still incapable of empirical exemplification. They are not necessary to the possession of any knowledge of objects. Thus Kant attributes them to the faculty of pure reason, as regulative concepts. They have a special role in human knowledge, but it is not that of referring to noumenal objects at all.

In this way, it is still possible for Kant to provide a solution for the antinomies along the same general lines as before. But it needs to be shown, in detail, how the pure concepts of understanding can be empirically exemplified—how they can be true of the phenomenal world, when they arise from the spontaneity of the intellect—and what exactly the role of the regulative concepts of reason is. These are the problems which were increasingly to occupy Kant's mind over the next few years, until at last they became so pressing that he postponed his projected *Metaphysic of Morals* (which was supposed to show 'the proper method of metaphysics', set the limits of the human faculties, and lay down the first principles of morality) in order to write the *Critique of Pure Reason*, in which he hoped to give them a definitive solution. (Cf. letters to Herder, dated 9 May 1767, but probably written 1768; and Lambert, 31 December 1765 and 2 September 1770; all in Ber. 10.)

It is the paradoxical conclusion of the *Dissertation*—that it precludes Newtonian science being true of the phenomenal world—which first makes clear the impossibility of maintaining that pure non-empirical concepts can give insight into the nature of a noumenal world. These concepts, in their supersensible use,

had to be denied objective reality, in order to provide the desired
metaphysical foundation for Newtonian science. This is one
central doctrine of the Critical philosophy, that, in their theoretical use, the demands of reason cannot be shown to be objectively
valid of transcendent reality. In its theoretical use, the principle
of sufficient reason remains entirely valid and forms the metaphysical grounding of the axioms of Newtonian science. But it is
valid only of the world of appearance, that world in which all
sensible qualities are modifications of inner sense and their
forms are only the inborn and subjective laws of the mind for
coordinating sensa.

3.8 THE ORIGINS OF THE CRITICAL VIEW OF ETHICS

Thus the 'two worlds' doctrine of the *Inaugural Dissertation* was
doomed to failure from the first; it, too, is a dream of metaphysics. But it does light the way to a more constructive, if
immanent role, for metaphysical thought to play than the *Dreams*
seemed to allow. And it marks a decisive stage in the development
of Kant's ethical thought, by clearly stating for the first time that
ethical concepts are known by the pure intellect, and not by moral
sense, even though they were still held to give knowledge of
noumenal reality.

Both the visionary dreams of Swedenborg, which attracted
and repelled different sides of Kant's character, and the dogmatic
dream of the *Inaugural Dissertation*, by means of which he hoped
to combine the major features of Wolffian rationalism with the
insights of inductive Newtonian science, had to be abandoned
before Kant could arrive at the well-known doctrine that the
moral law is a purely formal principle prescribed by reason to the
actions of empirical beings in the phenomenal world.

The *Dreams* and, to a lesser extent, the *Dissertation*, illuminate
the genesis of this view that morality derives from a reason which
is practical, and whose dictates are purely formal principles of
action. And they emphasise the importance of the vision of a
spiritual world in directing the development of Kant's ethical
thought. This is not to claim that what might be called 'Kantian
ethics' cannot be understood without appreciation of this background. But it should, I think, prepare the critic to take seriously
those parts of the ethical system which are often ignored or

glossed over (such as the 'Dialectic of Practical Reason') and to treat with suspicion those interpretations of Kant which present him as the stern advocate of 'duty for duty's sake', without consideration for human happiness or fulfilment. Any such interpretation would not accord well with the thought of a philosopher who was always predisposed to view man as a spiritual being with an eternal destiny and was thus always concerned above all with what constituted true human happiness and fulfilment.

The pre-Critical writings, even though Kant did not wish them to be included in his collected works,[4] show how essentially basic metaphysical views entered into the formulation of the Critical doctrine of ethics. It is part of my purpose to show that they remain essential even for the fully developed view; that Kant retained his early characterisation of morality and his belief in the spiritual context of morality, even though he thenceforth regarded speculative attempts to establish such views as nothing more than dreams.

[4] Cf. his instruction to his editor Tieftrunk, dated 13 October 1797: 'I assent with pleasure to your proposal for collecting and editing my minor writings. Only I wish you would not include writings earlier than 1770.' (Ber. 12, 206.)

CHAPTER FOUR

THE LECTURES ON ETHICS

4.1 THE ETHICAL DOCTRINE OF THE LECTURES

The development of the Critical philosophy from the dogmatism of the *Dissertation* has been well documented and I have nothing to add to already extant accounts (cf. de Vleeschauwer). But there is one important document from this period which bears directly on the crucial problem of the relation of metaphysics and ethics, and about which very little has been said by commentators in English.

This is the text of the *Lectures on Ethics*, which was compiled by Paul Menzer from manuscript notes of Kant's annual lectures, left by three students.[1] These are only compilations from notes, and Kant himself had a low opinion of the reliability of students' notes. Certainly, if they were all one had to work with, one could not claim for them a very high degree of accuracy in presenting Kant's lectures as they were actually delivered. But it must be borne in mind that many points are repeated, without substantial differences, at various places in the notes. Moreover, the doctrines are remarkably like those of the eventually published *Metaphysic of Morals*, and can be checked also against the second *Critique*, various extant reflections, fragments, and letters dated from about the same period.

If one does not treat them as magisterially authoritative, they do provide the best guide we have to Kant's developing ethical and metaphysical thought in the years 1775–81. And in general I think one is entitled to claim that they contain an accurate account of the substance of Kant's thinking, though their reliability is insufficient for deciding disputed questions of exact interpretation. One may even reasonably suppose that the material for Kant's projected but unwritten *Metaphysic of Morals* is contained in them.

[1] Some account of these sources is given by J. Macmurray in his Introduction to LE.

In the *Lectures*, Kant formulates a clear conception of the nature of 'practical philosophy' as a science which is concerned with the purely rational *a priori* laws governing the conduct of beings possessed of a free will. He draws a direct analogy between logic, which 'provides rules concerning the use of the understanding', and practical philosophy, providing rules for the use of the will. (LE, 2; Vor. 1 f.) Since moral obligation has a character of universality and necessity, it cannot be founded on any contingent fact such as 'moral feeling'. Such necessity must be founded on the spontaneous activity of the intellect, which legislates laws for a 'pure will' (a will not subject to empirical *determination*, though of course it will be affected by empirical inclinations). Such laws are perfectly general and 'have no regard to ends'. That is, they abstract from all particular ends, and state a principle the conformity to which has of itself 'inner worth'.

The principle governing such laws is what Kant variously (almost indifferently) calls 'consistency' and 'harmony'. It expresses, he says, 'the consistency of my free will with itself and with that of others; it is a necessary law of the free will'. (LE, 13; Vor. 17.) What Kant means by 'consistency' is not just lack of self-contradiction. It is more like a coherence in one's own conduct or with a harmonious social system of purposes. Thus he goes on to say, 'If the will is subordinated to the dictate of ends universally valid, it will be in harmony with all human purposes.' (LE, 17; Vor. 21.) The moral rules 'are derived from the universal ends of mankind', and so they 'give our actions universal validity and mould them into a general harmony'. (LE, 17; Vor. 22.) They provide a method for systematising the given empirical ends of our nature so as to make them 'universally valid', and thus harmonious and consistent.

In a reflection written between 1775–80 Kant writes, 'Freedom according to laws constitutes the form of the moral sense.' (S, 110; Ber. 19, 180.) The material is moral feeling, which 'has no other object than agreement with the purpose of humanity'. The intellect is here wholly limited to the phenomenal world, as the 'form of moral sense'. The formal law of morality, legislated by the intellect, allows only those ends which can be universally valid for all mankind and which effect a harmony of human purposes. But it then imposes their pursuit as unconditionally

E

obligatory. Virtue consists in pursuing this unconditional obligation for its own sake, despite the opposing power of particular inclinations. In pursuing virtue, one is asserting the dignity and worth of one's person as a rational being, above the animality of sensuous nature and the heteronomy (the external compulsion) of the inclinations. There is something of supreme value in the fact that man stands above nature and can act purely 'from duty'. Thereby he attains moral worth, becomes worthy of happiness and achieves self-mastery. This, rather than happiness itself, is the true end of man and his absolute value.

Kant's emphasis on the dignity of man leads him to adopt a characteristic view of particular duties. He stresses above all the virtue of honour, or respect for one's own person. He advocates proper pride, the avoidance of being put in the position of accepting favours (which puts one, he thinks, in an unrepayable debt), and steadfast courage. We must honour our persons by honouring our bodies and not putting them at the disposal of others. Duties both to oneself and others are based 'in the worth of manhood'. The whole value of the world lies in man's freedom from sensuous impulses. Freedom which is totally undetermined, however, 'is a terrible thing', worse even than empirical determination. Freedom, therefore, must be determined, not by sensibility, but by rules founded in the understanding; and these aim at the fulfilment of the greatest simultaneously possible number of 'the essential ends of humanity'. (LE, 122; Vor. 152.) Freedom is for the purpose of human fulfilment, and to use it otherwise is to contradict its nature. It is important to see that Kant is essentially concerned with the fulfilment of human purposes. His claim is simply that if these are determined by inclination, we act contrary to our essential, rational natures. Therefore they must be determined by freedom and its rules.

Kant's position emerges as a rather complex one, involving the notions of personal dignity, the harmony of human purposes, unity of will with itself and others, and the fulfilment of human nature. If one were forced to epitomise the view in a phrase an appropriate candidate might be: the infinite worth of social self-realisation through the free determination of sensuous nature. But it is doubtful whether all these strands can be forced into one principle at all. To this extent the *Lectures* may be said to benefit from their relative lack of systematisation within the Procrustean bed of the Kantian architectonic. All the most distinctive principles of Kantian ethics are represented here. But one can avoid awkward questions as to whether the different 'formulations of the categorical imperative' are really formulations of one principle or not; or of what Kant means by 'self-contradiction' in ethics; and one can see something of the wider context of a concern with perfection and happiness into which the formal conception of duty properly fits. For the *Lectures* deploy a less formal structure within which the varied and inter-relating strands of Kant's thought can often be seen more clearly.

To understand the complex interweaving of different strands of thought which were to be bound together into the formula of the categorical imperative, one needs to see the background metaphysical view of humanity as standing above nature, but with a destiny to realise itself in nature through struggle and discipline in a community of persons. Given such a view of himself, man needs to achieve proper self-respect—reverence for humanity in himself—which is the foundation of morality. The elements of this self-respect are humility, in view of one's inability to uphold the moral law or to maintain it in its purity even when one does conform to it; and 'true noble pride', in view of one's role as a representative of rational humanity and thus as standing above nature. This esteem for one's own moral worth is quite different from mere self-love. It is something which has infinite value and gives meaning to the pursuit of perfection in accordance with the precepts of morality. Kant summarises his general view in the aphorism that 'the end for which man is destined is to achieve his fullest perfection through his own freedom' (LE, 252; Vor. 317); and this will also be man's greatest happiness.

In view of what critics have sometimes said about the absence of a concern for personal happiness in Kant's ethics, one should note his final unequivocal declaration that 'God's will is that we should make ourselves happy' and that this is the true morality. (LE, 252: Vor. 317.) Without freedom, happiness and perfection would have been without moral worth. But the end of mankind is nevertheless natural and moral perfection—which is to be achieved through the struggle to virtue in face of one's natural inclinations, and which brings true happiness in its train.

4.2 VIRTUE AND HAPPINESS

The intimate relation adumbrated here between the concepts of virtue, perfection and happiness is clearly expressed in an unfinished fragment from the *Lose Blatter*, almost all of which is translated by Schilpp, who agrees with Menzer in dating it around 1775, though the date could be between 1771–84 (S, 127–30; Ber. 19, 276–82, no. 7202). This fragment is interesting in that it shows Kant at an intermediate stage between the *Inaugural Dissertation* and the *Groundwork*, struggling to formulate a coherent account of the relation between the intellectual basis of morality and the faculty of desire or moral feeling, by which the laws of understanding are given effect in the phenomenal world.

In this fragment Kant starts from the feeling of pleasure and asserts that *a priori* laws, derived from the understanding, 'contain the basis of a necessary delight for any rational being which has any capacity for desire'. (S, 127; Ber. 19, 276.) But how can pleasure be necessary for men when it depends, as he says, on their subjective constitutions? Kant's answer is provided by the assertion of the formal character of the laws in question. Just as the categories are formal principles for ordering sense-data in certain ways, so the moral laws are formal principles which allow certain sources of pleasure, rule out others and in general bring men's free choices of pleasures into 'agreement with themselves' and general harmony. Then, anything which is a possible basis of delight under such formal laws is 'good' and the delight in it is necessary for rational beings, and 'harmonises generally with happiness'. In this way 'the material of happiness is sensible, but its form is intellectual', and happiness becomes to some extent self-wrought, as man rises above the contingencies of nature, and finds pleasure in his measure of independence from and superiority to nature. (S, 127; Ber. 19, 276.) Kant speaks of morality (the '*a priori* unity of all the elements of happiness') as the original form (the formal element) of true happiness. Morality is a condition of the possibility of true happiness; but it is not a means to an independently conceived happiness.

Kant holds that a continuous sum of enjoyment is not necessary to happiness; nor are many evils of life incompatible with it. 'True' happiness must 'be derived from an *a priori* basis approved by reason'; and this may be termed a specific sort of happiness,

happiness-in-accordance-with-morality, or 'moral happiness'. (S, 128; Ber. 19, 277.) Moral happiness has intrinsic value; and 'Its inherent value consists of the fact that it is we who creatively produce it . . . it brings with it self-sufficiency', independence of empirical circumstances. (S, 128; Ber. 19, 277.)

Morality has this value, then, as the formal condition of the possibility of a specific sort of happiness. It is not the means to happiness, for a twofold reason. One does not first know the nature of the end to be achieved (what happiness will consist in) and then calculate the way to achieve it. And it cannot in fact be guaranteed to achieve the material element—pleasurable states—at least in this world.

On the other hand, morality is not an end in itself, in the sense that without any relation to anything other than itself and its own command it would have absolute worth. Morality, conformity to moral law, in which moral worth consists, is the formal condition of that sort of self-wrought happiness which alone finally deserves the name. Thus morality is 'a regulative principle of happiness *a priori*'; it determines 'the unity of the objects in an empirical happiness.' (S, 129; Ber. 19, 278.) In obeying the moral law for its own sake one is *ipso facto* aiming at the *a priori* specification of true moral happiness.

If one asks why this alone should be called 'true happiness' Kant's answer is in terms of the self-sufficiency of the human person which places it as metaphysically independent of and morally superior to nature. So, if one asks why it is moral to do what reason commands, in its formal principle of harmonious development, the answer lies in the intrinsic worth and dignity of the human personality, in its independence of all empirical grounds and its spontaneity of legislation—'freedom according to the laws of a thorough-going agreement with oneself . . . constitutes the worth and dignity of the person'. (S, 129; Ber. 19, 278.)

So Kant seems to hold in this fragment that happiness is naturally and rightly the motive to human action. But happiness is without value unless it is specified *a priori* by the formal principles of reason. Man must aim at a 'universal and necessary delight', existing within a harmonious system of ends. It is the moral law which imposes the formal principles which provide such universality and necessity. So reason has a constitutive role in creating human happiness, not a merely calculative task of estimating the probability of an independently conceived future happiness. It cannot be too strongly emphasised that the role of reason is a purely formal one and requires the material content of happiness to complete it, otherwise the moral law would be 'motiveless, arbitrary and absurd'. While the moral law must be obeyed for its own sake, the pursuit of morality requires the motive of happiness, a happiness determined *a priori* by reason. Thus Kant is able to say, 'happiness is a product of one's own human reason'. And again, 'the principle of self-sufficiency . . . is the condition of all happiness' and at the same time it determines man's absolute worth. (S, 130; Ber. 19, 281.)

4.3 THE MOTIVE TO MORAL ACTION

Although the fragment is obscure, unfinished and difficult, it is important for tracing the development of Kant's ethics. It emphasises the central place he gives to happiness as the material content of the moral life. And its notion of 'moral happiness' as a motive to morality exemplifies a transitional stage between moral sense theories and the rational formalism of the *Groundwork*.

In the *Lectures on Ethics* this notion is developed further. Kant thought that moral sense theorists had no difficulty in accounting for the practical, action-guiding force of moral principles though they could not account for the necessary character of moral obligation. Moral feelings, like many other sorts of feeling, are by nature able to 'move the will to perform action', and so they can be motives ('springs for the will which are drawn from the senses') (LE, 9; Vor. 12) or incentives to action. But in the *Dissertation* he founded the moral law on the intellect, not in feeling. And, he says, 'How the understanding can contain a principle of action is somewhat difficult to apprehend.' (LE, 44; Vor. 53.) His difficulty is expressed rather well in a letter to Herz of 1773, when he writes, 'The highest ground of morality . . . must itself please in the highest degree; for it is not merely a speculative representation, but must also have motive power.' (SPW, 120; Ber. 10, 138.) Even though intellectual in origin, morality must afford delight and must be able to act as an incentive of the will.

But Kant finds such a relation of intellect to sensibility very difficult to conceive: 'The understanding, obviously, can judge, but to give to this judgment a compelling force . . . that can move the will to perform the action—this is the philosopher's stone.' (LE, 45; Vor. 54.) He sees that the way of telling what duty is lies in the understanding. But, not yet having formed the notion of a reason which could of itself be practical, he feels the need to look elsewhere for the principle of our performance of duty, the 'subjective moral incentive'. And he still conceives that motive principle to be 'moral feeling'. (Cf. LE, 36; Vor. 44.)

As has been seen in the *Prize Essay* and the *Observations*, he uses the word 'feeling' very widely, to cover such diverse phenomena as a quasi-physiological urge to act, a sensation of desire, a 'feeling for the beauty and dignity of humanity', and the hope of or desire for future happiness—any psychological state, in effect, which might ordinarily be said to be an incentive for action. It is in this latter sense that Kant holds that 'theology is a motive for ethics'. (LE, 39; Vor. 48.) For only the existence of God and a life after death can assure one of that future happiness which is required as the motive to morality, but which is so uncertain and often impossible in this present life.

The doctrine which was hinted at in the *Dreams* is now explicitly stated, that though ethics cannot depend upon metaphysical or theological belief, nevertheless it necessarily gives rise to theological belief and cannot exist without it. 'To be ethical our conduct must involve a belief that God is holy and that He demands good dispositions from us.' (LE, 72; Vor. 90.) God's existence or volition does not make a certain act right; and knowledge of God is not required for us to know that it is right. But to impel us to perform the right action, in the face of sensuous obstacles, we need the motive of future (moral) happiness, which only the existence of God can guarantee.

We must perform a moral act because we judge it to be right. But what motivates us to perform it is faith that there is a judge of all things, i.e. there is ultimately a moral order in the universe, so that our present intentions will have real consequences for the sort of destiny we achieve. Acts have no moral worth if they are done simply because God commands them, out of fear of his power. But on the other hand, there is no point in doing what is seen to be objectively right if there is no incentive, in the form of future happiness, to do so; 'The divine will is the motive to action, not the ground of it.' (LE, 83; Vor. 104.)

In this discussion of the relation between feeling and understanding, in morality, Kant is wrestling with two main problems. In the first place, he is still puzzled as to how the purely formal role of reason can be related to substantive feelings of delight or impulses of the will—that is, how reason, which seems essentially theoretical in nature, can be practical, determining the will to action. Secondly, he is perplexed by the relation of moral rules, which legislate the *a priori* form of happiness, to the actual occurrence of happiness, which seems to depend on contingent empirical circumstances.

He attempts to solve both problems by distinguishing between the 'ground' of morality, which lies in rules of virtue, promulgated by reason and which is discerned by understanding; and the 'motive' to morality, which is the happiness of which virtuous conduct is worthy and which the existence of God guarantees. He also proposes that God is required as the 'ground of obedience' to morality. That is, though the understanding can discern what the moral law is, it is God who 'imposes upon everyone the obligation of acting in accordance with' the law. (LE, 52; Vor. 62.) It is God who presses the claim of obligation upon one, and makes it binding upon human wills. Here there is perhaps a hint of· the *Opus Postumum* doctrine that God and practical reason are to be identified. But Kant was still a long way from formulating that doctrine; and both these views, in this form, were to be short-lived. They were to be replaced by the Critical doctrine that reason just does of itself determine moral feeling ('reverence') and the will; and that happiness cannot be a motive to moral conduct. But though Kant abandoned the terminology of 'ground' and 'motive', the two later *Critiques*, the *Metaphysic of Morals* and the *Religion* all stress that morality cannot be entirely divorced from considerations of happiness; and that indeed one is still compelled to postulate 'happiness in accordance with morality' in order to render the categorical demands of the moral law intelligible. The fragment and the *Lectures* remain important sources for a just appreciation of what Kant might have meant by this rather mysterious doctrine, which has often been simply jettisoned as an irrelevant blunder by commentators. And they show that the doctrine was from the first a central and important concern· for Kant, rather than some sort of afterthought to propitiate religious believers.

4.4 GOD AND DUTY

A fairly large section of the *Lectures on Ethics* is devoted to the doctrine of religion, and as well as being independently interesting as an account of Kant's attitude to religion, it helps to make more explicit the general metaphysical background which forms the context for his developing ethical theory.

As one would expect, he strongly rejects any suggestion that acts are right only because God commands them. 'If . . . the reason why I ought not to lie were that God had forbidden it . . . then it would follow that He might have refrained from forbidding it.' (LE, 22; Vor. 27.) In other words such a doctrine would undermine the necessary character of morality. Nevertheless, God, as the perfect being and as purely intellectual, is by nature morally good—i.e. 'the dispositions of the divine mind . . . are in accordance with objective morality and action which is objectively moral is thus in conformity with the divine will'. (LE, 23; Vor. 29.)

The divine will by necessity of its nature acts according to rational law; and this is because it is solely and supremely rational. It is not that goodness is a standard to which God must conform. It is rather that goodness is simply what a rational will necessarily wills, when unconditioned by sensuous impulses. But this does not entail that God must exist as the basis of morality, i.e. that a perfectly pure rational will must exist if morality is to be possible. For the concept of a divine will may only be an Idea of reason, not exemplified in any reality, a hypothetical limiting case of actual, imperfectly rational, human wills. The necessary character of morality is founded in the laws of the activity of a purely rational will, not in the necessity of the being of God.

Kant also refuses to allow any doctrine of revelation in morals. Though he constantly affirms that the Gospels are the best presentation of pure morality there is, he also constantly asserts that 'the moral law is holy not because it has been revealed to us . . . our own reason is capable of revealing it to us. This fact makes us ourselves judges of the revelation'. (LE, 75; Vor. 93.) Indeed, we only decide that it is God who has revealed something to us by applying moral criteria to putative revelations— 'We recognise the perfection of the divine will from the moral law.' (LE, 40 f.; Vor. 49.)

Similarly, even if there are examples of a morally good life, 'The examples themselves can only be judged good or bad by reference to universal principles. The archetype lies in the understanding.' (*Loc. cit.*) Jesus therefore cannot be the archetype or exemplar of the perfect moral life. To know whether his life is perfect or not we must judge it by the rules of morality which already exist in our minds. Whereas his life may 'serve for our encouragement and emulation', it can never be taken as a revelation of true morality. So, Kant concludes, the only important thing in religion is that which is common to all religions, obedience to the moral law and hope of grace to remedy man's seemingly inevitable moral deficiencies. Beyond this a man may believe what he pleases, as long as he does not regard the specific observances of his own religion as in themselves an especially pleasing service to God, or as any more than 'a means of awakening within us a godly disposition'.

Kant admits a certain value to devotional exercises but not as ends in themselves—he has no time for the worship, or as he calls it, the 'flattery' of God. Devotions may be useful as means 'to make the knowledge of God work effectually upon the will'. They are thus methods of self-help, and their object is not an external being, God, but one's own future conduct: 'Devotional exercises are meant for the purpose of acquiring the habit of doing good.' (LE, 89; Vor. 112.) All men may honour God by obeying the moral law, but not by praise. And all may love God by taking pleasure in doing his commandments, not by having imaginary fellowship with him.

We praise God only by using our conception of his perfections 'as a ground of impulse to awaken in us dispositions to practical goodness'. (LE, 113; Vor. 141.) Our souls may thus be strengthened and invigorated by such contemplation of the divine perfections; but again contemplation is not an end in itself. Praise is 'of subjective but of no objective value . . . we do not profit God by uttering His praises'. (*Loc. cit.*)

Naturally, Kant has not much time for public worship. The way to attain what he calls an intuition of the greatness of God is not by singing hymns, he says, but by being 'led to appreciate the works of God' in nature. He writes that a righteous man will feel shame, if surprised at his devotions, and that 'there is something pathetic . . . in praying in church'. (LE, 115; Vor.

144.) This feeling he attributes to the fear of hypocrisy, and the tendency of prayer to turn God, the proper object of faith, into an object of intuition. It may well be thought that many of Kant's strictures on public religious observances sprang from emotional reaction to his over-rigorous Pietistic upbringing rather than from dispassionate speculation.

The same reaction against the sort of Protestant piety which claims intimate familiarity with God is to be found in his peculiar abhorrence of the notion of personal communion with God. 'Fanaticism', he says, 'is an illusion of the inner sense whereby we believe ourselves to be in fellowship with God and with other spirits.' (LE, 103; Vor. 129.) Again, 'To wish to converse with God is absurd . . . we cannot intuit God.' (LE, 99; Vor. 123.) He remarks that perhaps 'the highest moral perfection would . . . consist in communion with the Supreme Being'; but this is an ideal which is beyond our reach, and so an ethics which is based on an ideal so disproportionate to human nature is 'fanciful and visionary'. (LE, 78; Vor. 97 f.)

In these doctrines the strange, almost inconsistent, humanism of Kant comes to the fore. While he is concerned not to renounce one jot of the purity of the moral law because of the weakness of man's nature and has to appeal to divine help to make up this weakness and to assure man of future fulfilment and happiness, yet he will not countenance any conception of an immanent work of grace or of mystical union with God. Again this perhaps expresses a reaction against the Pietist doctrines of sanctification through grace and personal fellowship with the Lord. But it also shows his reluctance to give religious concepts an immanent role in the moral life, and his tendency to relegate them to a subsidiary role, as an external addition to an autonomously conceived morality. Here is reflected an inherent instability of Kant's ethics —its uneasy tread between humanism and religion—which is responsible for so many of the difficulties critics find in it.

4.5 MORALITY AND RELIGION

In the *Lectures* Kant is already expressing in a developed form the views on religion which were to be later published in the *Religion*. Two letters to J. C. Lavater, a Swiss poet and admirer of Kant's who asked for his opinion on a book on faith and prayer, dated 1775, corroborate the views which are recorded in the *Lectures*. Kant writes that he distinguishes the teachings of Christ from the reports we have of those teachings. And he assumes that the teaching consisted of moral doctrines as opposed to dogmas: 'Dogmas tell only what God has done to help us see our frailty', whereas the truly important thing is the moral law itself. (KPC, 80; Ber. 10, 168.) Here we have no need of special revelation. We know the holiness of the law and the 'insuperable evil of our hearts'. And all we need to add is that if we do whatever is in our power, God will in some unknown way supplement our deficiencies.

We should trust God, therefore, not harbouring 'any inquisitive desire to know how His purposes will be achieved' (*loc. cit.*), nor any 'presumptuous confidence' that salvation will follow our acceptance of the Gospel. In this respect Kant rejects the Pietist belief in the certain assurance of salvation by faith alone and insists that the 'pure fundamental teachings' of the Gospels are concerned with moral faith. This is the confidence that having sought righteousness with all our might, we may have 'unconditional trust that God will then supplement our efforts and supply the good that is not in our power', though we do not know how. (KPC, 83; Ber. 10, 171.) This, Kant avers, is the only true religion, the central core of Christianity, which dispenses with miracles, revelations, prayer and 'the so-called worship that religious fanaticism always demands'. (KPC, 80; Ber. 10, 169.)

Kant states that he is prepared to put his trust in any means of reconciliation which is revealed—or in any other means, unrevealed to men. For such knowledge of *how* God perfects man does not in the least make one a better person; and one can never be so arrogant as to say that any means is the only one to attain perfection. In other words, *what* God does is of no concern to man's life; only that he does something. The moral man will thus refrain from deciding on the truth of what is remote in time and faintly evidenced, and concern himself only with moral effort, together with a morally inspired hope. The specific Christian revelation has nothing to contribute to the moral life of man; but 'anyone can be convinced of the correctness and necessity of moral faith' which is rather derogated from than added to by veneration of Jesus or 'the wooing of favour by the performing of rituals'. (KPC, 81; Ber. 10, 169. KPC, 83; Ber. 10, 172.)

Thus, although Kant says that 'in religion all our morality ought to reach its fulfilment in respect of its object', he does not have much place for revealed religion in his scheme. (LE, 79; Vor. 98.) He holds that its function is to bring in 'the factor of higher divine aid'—that is, it states how man's moral deficiencies are to be made up by God. But 'no man can hope for supernatural help unless he behaves as he naturally ought to' (LE, 84; Vor. 105); and revealed religion is in no way necessary to man's moral life now or indeed his salvation hereafter.

There are, nevertheless, two ways in which natural religion, as opposed to revealed religion, essentially and necessarily enters into the true conception of morality. First, since our actions continually fall short of the requirements of the moral law, man would in the long run have to give up observing such a law, if it were not for 'his belief that his moral insufficiency will be made good by Heaven'. (LE, 92; Vor. 115.) The first part of religious belief is that Heaven will make up the moral deficiencies of the worthy. The second part, 'which is to be regarded merely as a consequence of the first, is that if we have so behaved we may hope for reward'. Religion is required to help man attain a pure moral will and to assure him of an appropriate happiness.

Because of these features of divine supplementation and judgment, Kant regards atheism as undermining morality, by 'depriving it of motive power'; though sometimes, he says, a man may simply not realise the necessity of the postulate of God; or he may be a theist in practice though not in theory. Such men are deceived by speculative error. What they need to know is the primacy of practical reason and the necessity of its postulates. From these comments, it seems that Kant does not regard the concept of God as a necessary motivation to morality in the sense that one must explicitly believe in God before one can be moral. He means that a fully reflective account of morality must issue in the postulate of God, if it is to justify the moral beliefs of the plain man, pure in heart; 'Otherwise the mind can form no conceptions, either of the order of the purposive, nor can it apprehend the ground of obedience to the moral law.' (LE, 87; Vor. 108.) Conscious atheism, he holds, 'amounts to a decision to set aside the principles of the moral law'. So one may put aside all theological controversy about God and ignore all books concerned with such controversy. One must then rest a confident faith only in what is necessary to give one's moral obedience worth and validity.

In this respect Kant repeats the traditional impersonal theism of rationalist philosophers throughout history. God is the metaphysical ground of all being, not a supreme person. What Kant adds to the rationalist picture is that we are committed to such a ground only in such a way and to the extent that its assertion is a necessary postulate of conceiving the moral life as we do. God remains a remote and impassive being, for Kant: 'We cannot affect God in any way.' (LE, 104; Vor. 130.) Towards Him we must be reverent, *qua* law-giver; loving, *qua* beneficent ruler; and fearful, *qua* just judge. Such attitudes are not expressed primarily in ceremony, but simply in living the moral life rightly. They are attitudes to which we are committed in being committed to morality, and in this sense are implicit in a true view of morality itself.

In line with this general conception Kant rules out belief in particular acts of providence: 'The ways of God are the divine intentions which determine the government of the world. We should not seek to define these in detail.' (LE, 94; Vor. 118.) God's intentions and purposes are universal in their nature, and so 'universal nature, not particular circumstances, ought to evoke our thankfulness'. God does not interfere in the course of nature to grant us special favours. Thus intercessory prayer for particular matters is misdirected and even presumptuous. We must resign ourselves to the general will of God in the belief that it is directed to the final moral purpose of all things, but not regard particular events which happen to us as either divine graces or punishments.

Clearly Kant's account of religion is alien to the traditional Christian notions of special acts of God in history and personal experience and special revelation by God in Christ. But it is equally clear that the views he holds on the nature of morality arise within the context of general metaphysical beliefs about the nature of the world and God, and lose much of their point when abstracted from that context. His insistence on the absoluteness of duty, man's moral insufficiency and the hope of divine help and ultimate happiness makes his ethical doctrine unmistakably religious in tone. So, if Kant seems to reduce theological utterances to moral assertions, yet his moral doctrine is itself, perhaps largely unconsciously, imbued with a religious view of life.

4.6 THE IMPORTANCE OF THE LECTURES

The *Lectures on Ethics* can be seen to represent an intermediate stage in the development of the final Critical view of ethics; and they are valuable in three main respects.

First, the very imprecision of the terminology and relative looseness of structure of the text helps to bring out the complexities of Kant's doctrine, its many-strandedness, in a way that the explicit concern of the *Groundwork* with the formulation of one supreme principle of morality may obscure.

Second, the *Lectures* show the central place of the notion of 'happiness' in Kant's ethics, and express his early attempts to find a terminology which could relate the concepts of virtue, happiness and perfection in an integral unity. Kant found these attempts—seeing morality as the *a priori* form of happiness, or happiness (through God) as the motive to morality—unsatisfactory. As will be suggested, the development of ethical formalism prevented him from finding a more satisfactory terminology. But one can see in these early formulations the first stages of Kant's doctrine of the postulates of practical reason. And one can see that they are not peripheral, but absolutely central to his developing conception of the nature of morality.

Third, the *Lectures* clearly express Kant's central concern with what may be called the natural theology of morals, the metaphysical background which is partly presupposed by and partly founded upon the notion of a rational morality for sensuous beings.

One of the things I wish to bring out in this study is the deep instability in Kant's final doctrine which arises from his retention of an essentially religious view of morality, together with the development of a terminology of pure formalism, which prevents him from making religion more than an unknowable supplement to morality. Not until the *Opus Postumum* is this instability explicitly recognised, and religion given an integral place in the conception of morality itself. But at any stage of his thought it is only a one-sided view which can ignore the metaphysical or religious dimension entirely, and claim to provide an adequate account of Kant's ethics without reference to distinctive doctrines of God and the Self. Some doctrine of man as unconditioned by the sensory world and of God as the ultimate ground of the unity of the sensory and intelligible worlds, is required for Kant's ethics to have initial plausibility. Not to have seen this is, I suspect, not to have seen Kant in historical context.

CHAPTER FIVE

THE CRITICAL DOCTRINES OF GOD AND THE SELF

5.1 THE DOCTRINE OF THE SELF

Kant's Critical philosophy, as expressed in the *Critique of Pure Reason* (First Edition in Ber. 4; Second Edition in Ber. 3), has been expounded and criticised at length by many scholars, and I shall assume that it is familiar to readers of this volume. But it is necessary to comment briefly upon two topics which are of central importance to his ethical theory; namely, the doctrine of the self's transcendence of the empirical world and the complex account of theistic language which is the basis of the doctrine of the postulates of practical reason. Without these doctrines, Kant's ethical views must seem largely unintelligible; and this fact again argues for the recognition of a close interdependence between Kant's ethical and metaphysical thought.

The doctrine of the self is mainly developed in the Paralogisms of pure reason and the Third Antinomy, and it expresses very well the great complexity—some would say the incoherence—of the Critical doctrine. That doctrine explicitly restricts the meaningful use of the categories to phenomena, and thus limits knowledge to possible data of 'intuition', or sense-experience. So if there is to be any knowledge of the self, it can only be knowledge of the self as an object of experience, as appearance. In one sense Kant does say that 'the soul' is simply to be identified with the whole complex of representations which form the basis of human knowledge, and which all 'belong, in themselves, as determinations of the mind to our inner state'. (A, 34; B, 50.)

Kant makes it clear in the *Inaugural Dissertation* that all the sense-representations which form the material content of human knowledge are simply 'modifications of inner sense'. That is, since they are spatio-temporal phenomena, and since the forms of space and time are created by the mind itself, there is a sense in

F

which the whole material content of knowledge is dependent for its specific nature upon the subjective constitution of the human mind. In particular, while only some objects of knowledge have spatial characteristics, and so belong to 'outer sense', all possible objects of human knowledge—including feelings and various psychological states—are temporal in character, and so belong to 'inner sense'. As objects of human knowledge—as appearances—they exist within the formal framework of time, which is produced by the activity of the mind itself. In this way they come to be spoken of by Kant as 'modifications of inner sense'. And 'the soul' or 'self' may be understood as the complete set of representations which modify one unified 'inner sense'—one temporal framework of experience. The self, on this understanding, just *is* the unity of various elements in one consciousness.

This notion approximates to the Humean view of the self as a bundle of impressions and ideas: 'We know nothing but our mode of perceiving objects—a mode which is peculiar to us.' (A, 42; B, 59.) The self, in this sense, is known in what Kant calls empirical self-consciousness, which 'is in itself diverse and without relation to the identity of the subject'. (B, 133.) That is, there is no fixed or abiding element of inner sense, which could give rise to an intuition of a self. So it may seem that the concept of the self becomes identified with the notion of a certain sort of unity among sense-contents, by which they are members of one consciousness, or determinations of one 'inner sense'.

However, Kant also develops, especially in the 'Subjective Deduction', the notion of the self as a non-empirical source of the active faculties of imagination, understanding and reason, which can only be known in its manner of uniting intuitions according to concepts so as to make knowledge possible. Knowledge, for Kant, is not simply a passive registering of appearances, as if on a blank screen. On the contrary, it requires various complex mental activities as its preconditions. The forms of space and time must themselves be produced, and sensa (to use Kant's term from the *Inaugural Dissertation*) must be organised within those forms. Then the mind must discriminate various sensa from each other, interpret them in terms of conceptual categories so that they provide knowledge of objects and combine them into the unity of one consciousness. All these mental acts seem to require the concept of an agent intellect which can combine, unite and distinguish sensa in accordance with concepts. And so 'the self' becomes more than the bundle of representations; it becomes that the spontaneous activity of which makes any knowledge possible.

One can never, it is true, have an intuition of this self; but it is known in its activity of synthesising, combining and uniting representations into the unity of one consciousness. This notion could perhaps still be given a phenomenalist interpretation, and one could regard the sense of spontaneity and cognitive activity, which, Kant holds, is involved in all knowing, as simply one distinguishable aspect within experience, which contrasts with a complementary aspect of passivity, or 'giveness'.[1] One might still say that there is no transcendent self, but only a distinction to be made within experience between mental activity and passivity. Many phrases seem to support this view; as when Kant says that the 'I think' is just a 'form of apperception [self-consciousness], which belongs to and precedes every experience'. (A, 354.) Such a sense of spontaneity may indeed be present throughout the whole experience of a certain person. But it need not show that there is some further transcendent cause of this spontaneity. The sense of acting, and of knowing an object, can be distinguished from the sense of being acted upon. But this, it may be said, is a distinction which arises *within* experience; it is a 'purely formal' distinction which does not require any further explanation in terms of a transcendent cause.

Yet Kant does undoubtedly write of a 'subject-in-itself', which as substratum underlies this 'I' (cf. A, 350), and of which we can have no knowledge. There is, he seems to hold, a real transcendent ground of spontaneity. Just as the noumenal world of things-in-themselves is the unknowable transcendent ground of the sense-contents which the intellect discriminates, remembers and recognises; so the mental acts of discriminating and recognising are attributed to a non-spatio-temporal source which manifests itself in such acts of spontaneity. But one cannot say whether this source is one or many, permanent or transient, simple or complex in nature; or, indeed, whether the transcendent grounds of the self and of sensa are the same, or different. One can speak only of the internal unity of experience and of the mental spontaneity

[1] Cf. P. F. Strawson, *Individuals*, ch. 2; where he elaborates such a possibility. (Methuen, London, 1959.)

involved in all knowing: 'I exist as an intelligence which is conscious solely of its power of combination.' (B, 158.)

Though Kant claims, consistently with the Critical doctrine, that nothing whatsoever can be known of the transcendent ground of spontaneity, he does nevertheless continually speak of it in definite ways—as 'absolute unity', 'intelligence' and 'spontaneity'. So a further interpretation of the doctrine appears—not that there is no transcendent self and not that, though there is one, nothing can be known of it; but that, while not having knowledge of the self, there are nevertheless correct ways of *thinking* about it. Though one cannot see how our concepts find application in a non-spatio-temporal world, and so cannot know the transcendent self, one must yet think of it as if it had certain features. One must think in these ways, however, solely for heuristic reasons. The soul must be conceived as a substance, simple in nature and numerically one throughout all experience; but only in order to provide an ideal of absolute and systematic unity for psychological investigation (cf. B, 700). The correct way of thinking of the transcendent reality of the self is the way which best guides empirical investigation into psychological phenomena. As Kant puts it, such concepts of the transcendent have a purely 'immanent use'. This fourth conception seems the most likely candidate for the title of the Critical doctrine of the self; and, as we shall see (5.3 and 5.4), it closely parallels Kant's account of language about God.

Kant's rather complex doctrine is clearly meant to rule out two contrasting alternative views. First, a rationalist metaphysics which takes the substantial soul to be an immaterial thing; which asserts that the soul must be conceived as a simple enduring substance, and regards 'simplicity' as entailing incorruptibility (since what is simple is indissoluble); and which takes 'unity' as a proof of personal identity. In these ways, rational psychology arrives at the doctrine that the unitary, simple, substantial self is a spiritual, enduring, incorruptible being. Against such a view, which Kant had himself propounded in the pre-Critical writings, he now asserts that the 'I' is simply a function expressing the unity and mental spontaneity which is necessarily involved in all thought and action. Such a purely logical 'principle of apperception' cannot be used to justify the existence of the self as one identical thing, enduring through time. 'We are unable from our

own consciousness to determine whether, as souls, we are permanent or not.' (A, 364.) From the fact that 'I' accompanies all my
representations, no inferences can be drawn to 'my' numerical
identity, as a subject-self, or to my possible persistence after
bodily death.

We can speak of the 'I think', which accompanies all our
knowledge, not as a phenomenon, but as a 'formula of our
consciousness'. But this is not a concept of an identifiable entity,
and so it can never give rise to objective knowledge. There is a
necessary unity in experience, which makes all one's experiences
experiences *of* one subject; but this 'logical point' does not establish the reality of one enduring substantial self. Kant's point
might be put in different terminology by saying that all experiences
are experiences *of* a subject. It is a necessary condition of identi-
fying, and thus of having knowledge of, an experience, that it
should be thought of as belonging to a person. Moreover, the
relation of an experience to the person who 'owns' it is logically
non-transferable, in that an experience of person X could not
logically become an experience of person Y. It is thus a necessary
condition of talking of experiences as we do, that all experiences
should be related to some 'subject of experiences'; and that they
should be related in a logically non-transferable way, so as to
form part of a 'unity of experience' which is in some sense
necessary.

However, this admission goes no way to establishing that there
exists one enduring substantial self. Numerical identity requires
the permanence of an object in a spatio-temporal framework (cf.
B, 420). But the 'subject of experiences' may perhaps pass from
one substance to another, as Locke suggests. Then, though the
unity of experience would remain, the person, as an observable
identifiable substance, would have changed. Thus, though we
necessarily judge ourselves to be 'the same' subject of experiences
throughout our lives, we cannot prove that this subject is not
itself in a state of continual flux. More precisely, it is senseless to
speak of it as either permanent or impermanent; for the 'I' itself
is a function expressing the related unity of all thoughts in one
consciousness, not an object at all. The basic mistake of rational
psychology, Kant holds, is that it treats the unity which is the
ground of all knowledge as the unity of an enduring object. But
the subject of experiences cannot be known as an object at all ('I

do not know myself through being conscious of myself as thinking' (B, 406)); and *a fortiori* it cannot be asserted to be an
immaterial, incorruptible, enduring object.

But if such metaphysical claims to establish a 'spiritualism' of
the soul are ruled out, any form of materialism is excluded even
more firmly. Kant says, 'If I remove the thinking subject the
whole corporeal world must at once vanish' (A, 383); for that
world is nothing but a mode of representation in the sensibility
of the subject (cf. A, 42; A, 114; A, 129). Even though we have no
knowledge of the self as object; though it may be inseparable from
the physical world as we perceive it; though it may manifest one
world-soul or many incorruptible substances, or something totally
mysterious; nevertheless, the assertion that there is a transcendent
ground of the unity of consciousness and of the mental acts of
discrimination and recognition decisively excludes materialism—
the view that consciousness is, at best, an epiphenomenon or by-
product of material processes. And so it keeps open the bare
logical possibility of a non-empirical source of human action and
of a sort of immortality (though Kant is careful to deny that he has
proved such a source to be a real, as opposed to a logical, possibility).

Immortality would be, Kant suggests, the continuation of the
unity of one's experience in a differently intuited world; 'those
transcendental objects, which in our present state appear as
bodies, could be intuited in an entirely different manner'. (A,
394.) So it may be possible 'to hope for an independent and continuing existence of my thinking nature, throughout all possible
change of my state', and even throughout a change to a totally
different mode of intuiting objects. (A, 383.) Kant here echoes
Swedenborg's doctrine that after death we do not move to a
different sphere. We see the same world, but not in its character
as appearance; rather, we see things as they really are. Of course,
this possibility can neither be established nor disconfirmed
theoretically. So Kant comes to the general conclusion that we
should 'divert our self-knowledge from fruitless and extravagant
speculation to fruitful practical employment'. (B, 421.) The
establishment of speculative agnosticism leaves the way clear for a
positive doctrine founded on moral considerations.

5.2 THE FREEDOM OF THE SELF

I have suggested that the Critical doctrine of the self is that it must be asserted to be a transcendent reality, of which no knowledge can be claimed; but which must be thought of in terms of certain concepts which have an immanent, heuristic and regulative function in interpreting experience. One such regulative function is to guide the investigations of psychologists; and this does not seem very compelling today.[2] But another set of ways of conceiving the transcendent nature of the self is founded on moral experience, and this is the one with which Kant is chiefly concerned.

He sets out the theoretical foundation for his doctrine in the Third Antinomy of reason, concerned with freedom and deterministic causality. Holding that reason can prove both that every event must have a cause and that there must be an uncaused cause to begin every causal series, Kant proposes that both apparently contradictory assertions can be true of the same phenomenon, considered from different points of view. One and the same event, as appearance, can be necessarily determined according to law; but as intelligible reality (or what he calls the 'transcendent object') it may stand outside the causal series and be itself 'an absolute totality of conditions determining causal relation' (A, 533; B, 561), an uncaused cause of all relevant events in the spatio-temporal realm.

Kant is careful to stress that this is no proof that there is such a noumenal freedom, which is itself unconditioned but is yet the ground of temporal causal sequences. But he holds that the concept of freedom is a necessary concept of reason, which always seeks for absolute spontaneity, unity and totality. And it does not appear to be self-contradictory. The argument does not, however, show that such a concept of noumenal freedom expresses a real possibility, as opposed to being 'an empty thought concept'. But, Kant holds, it is a concept which man must suppose to be instantiated, in order to regulate his actions in accordance with the demands of morality. For 'If appearances are things in themselves, freedom cannot be upheld.' (A, 536; B, 564.) We must in practice presuppose that we are free from empirical determination,

[2] Cf. P. F. Strawson, *The Bounds of Sense* (Methuen, London, 1966), p. 160.

to justify our sense of moral obligation and responsibility. The ideal of freedom cannot, like the ideal of absolute totality in the case of the mathematical antinomies, be simply a heuristic ideal towards which one must strive. For even to begin moral striving one must presuppose that freedom is a fact (cf. A, 547; B, 575). So man must regard himself as both empirically determined and intelligibly free, in so far as he regards himself as a moral agent.

In the first *Critique*, it seems that Kant believed that noumenal spontaneity could be attributed to man not only on moral grounds, but in respect of the faculties of reason and understanding. Man, he says, 'knows himself through pure apperception . . . in acts and inner determinations which he cannot regard as impressions of the senses'. (A, 546; B, 574.) Reason determines the understanding by means of ideas, which in turn determines the world by means of pure concepts. In respect of reason and understanding, man thus knows himself as a 'purely intelligible object', a ground of ideas and pure concepts, which cannot derive from the empirical world. Nor are these faculties objects of sensible intuition; yet they cause effects in the world. So the understanding serves as a 'sensible sign' of the non-empirical ground of determinations which man must conceive himself to be (cf. A, 546; B, 574). The activities of thinking and reflection, Kant suggests, enable one to justify the attribution of noumenal freedom to the agent.

Kant repeats this 'deduction' of the concept of freedom in the third section of the *Groundwork*. But by the time of the second *Critique* he had become more sceptical about speaking of speculative reason as licensing the postulate of freedom. This scepticism, however, never extended to practical reason; and even for the most sceptical form of the Critical philosophy, the demands of morality, which issue from practical reason and categorically impose the obligation to act in certain ways upon man, require that he should at least *represent* reason as having a non-empirical causality which can enable him to do what duty demands (cf. A, 547; B, 575).

Reason, conceived as noumenally free, cannot stand under any conditions of time, and it must therefore be thought of as changeless and eternal. 'No action begins *in* this active being itself; but we may yet quite correctly say that the active being *of itself* begins its effects in the sensible world.' (A, 541; B, 569.) That is, the whole temporal world of appearances is non-temporally dependent upon the unchanging free noumenal act.

Thus Kant can write, in the *Critique of Practical Reason*, that all the empirical actions of a man 'belong to a single phenomenon of his character, which he himself creates, and according to which he imputes to himself . . . the causality of that appearance'. (CPR, 101; Ber. 5, 98.) Again, 'The entire chain of appearances . . . depends upon the spontaneity of the subject as a thing-in-itself.' (CPR, 103; Ber. 5, 99.) Consequently, a man is responsible even for his empirically conditioned character, however contingently determined it may seem; for he is the ground of all his circumstances!

In spite of the Critical doctrine of the limitation of knowledge to appearances, Kant ends by speaking of the self as a spiritual member of an intelligible realm, a unitary ground of spontaneity which possesses legislative authority, in both knowledge and action, over the whole material world of phenomena. But, dogmatic as this language sounds, Kant continues to hold that it does not express knowledge of the real, intelligible ground of appearances. The visionary doctrine of the *Theory of the Heavens* and the *Dreams* has become transmuted into a set of postulates or 'models' for conceiving an unknowable transcendent reality, for the purpose of 'the determination of the Subject and its volition' (B, 166n); and particularly for determining the will to moral action. Man must conceive himself to be a noumenally free determining ground of empirical nature, in order to render his experience of moral obligation intelligible to himself.

5.3 THE CONCEPT OF GOD

Just as the early rationalist doctrine of the self is denied speculative validity, but admitted as a practical postulate of morality; so the early rationalist doctrine of God is retained, but solely for practical use, without any cognitive function. That doctrine, as shown in section 1.3, is basically that God is a necessary being who is also the *Ens Realissimum*, the sum-total—or, as Kant prefers to put it, the 'ground'—of all possible predicates. All finite beings arise by limitation of the *Ens Realissimum* in various ways (cf. A, 578; B, 606); for he contains in himself, or

conditions the possibility of, all particular things. In the first
Critique, Kant retains this notion of an all-real being, an individual completely determined by ideas alone, which 'serves as
basis for the complete determination that necessarily belongs to
all that exists'. (A, 576; B, 604.) But he holds that reason presupposes not the existence of such a totality of all possible
predicates in one individual but only the idea of it; and only 'for
the purpose of deriving from an unconditioned totality the conditioned totality'. (A, 578; B, 606.)

Kant entitles this idea the ideal of reason, and finds its source
in reason itself. Reason is not concerned directly with objects but
solely with the faculty of understanding; its function is to regulate
the rules of understanding to form the greatest possible systematic
totality of knowledge, 'to find for the conditioned knowledge
obtained through the understanding the unconditioned whereby
its unity is brought to completion'. (A, 307; B, 364.) The ideal of
God is an asymptotic principle, positing a regulative goal which
will never be finally reached, the goal of the complete determination of everything by the assignation to it of one of each pair
of contradictory predicates out of the actual sum of all possible
predicates. The concept of God represents this totality of all
possibility, and 'is itself undetermined in respect of the predicates
which may constitute it'. (A, 573; B, 601.) It is, properly speaking, just a model which suggests a fruitful rule for the employment of understanding, in aiming at the complete, exhaustive
determination of all realities.

In a similar way the idea of a necessary being is posited by
reason as the idea of an unconditioned reality upon which all
conditioned things depend (cf. A, 584; B, 612). We may go on to
form the 'optional assumption' of the real existence of such a
being, 'entirely outside the series of the sensible world'. (A, 561;
B, 589.) But we are not speculatively justified in doing so; and
for all we know the concept 'may be in itself impossible'. (A, 562;
B, 590.) We can certainly form no positive notion of a necessary
being and so we may be thinking nothing at all; speculatively we
just cannot tell. Kant explicitly retracts his early ontological
proof of God by saying that the concept of a being which, when
removed together with all its predicates, leaves a self-contradiction, is an unintelligible one. There is nothing the non-existence
of which is self-contradictory; though one cannot, he says, infer

from this the impossibility of a being the existence of which is necessary: 'I can remove in thought every existing substance . . . but I cannot infer from this . . . that their non-existence is possible.' (A, 244; B, 302.) So all the proof from the Fourth Antinomy shows is that the concept of a necessary being is not, as far as we can tell, self-contradictory; not that it is necessary, actual or even possible in itself. The idea enables understanding to trace a systematic, universal and necessary unity among entities in the world by connecting them, in thought, with an imagined ultimate ground. The idea is purely subjective, a formal condition of thinking; though it is not impossible, so far as we know, that it may also have some sort of reference to noumenal reality.

A third strand in the concept of God is the notion of an intellectual intuition, which knows things as they are, not just as they appear; which is not discursive, gradually increasing its knowledge by means of ever-extending comparisons of similar phenomena throughout a period of time, but knows each particular immediately, instantaneously and fully; and which itself creates the objects of its knowledge. Kant mentions this notion repeatedly throughout the first *Critique*, and holds that it arises by contrast with the notion of a discursive intuition like the human understanding. Yet since the notion must be formulated in terms of the categories, and since they are essentially forms of discursive thought—'functions of unity in judgment'—Kant is forced to say that they are necessarily inapplicable, even as forms of thought, when applied to a transcendent God. Thus not only is talk of God 'empty' or purely formal—being not founded on sense-perceptions—it is necessarily inapplicable to the object it attempts to conceive. So there is no question that a noumenal object might *correspond* to these ideas of reason. The transcendent may be unknowable; but the Critical doctrine of the formal nature of the categories of thought and their restriction to the role of functions of discursive thought requires that our concepts actually be denied any literal application to transcendent reality.

The fourth strand in Kant's concept of God is that of the wise, benevolent designer of nature; the necessary, omniscient ground of all possibilities is thereby construed also as a supremely intelligent cause. Kant holds that we must 'assume a wise and omnipotent author of the world'. (A, 698; B, 726.) This is not, however, an inductive, speculative inference from observed data to their unobserved cause. For to prove a creator rather than merely an architect or group of architects from the order in nature requires some form of cosmological proof to a necessary ground of contingent being. And to determine this creator as supreme in all possible perfections requires an ontological proof from the concept of a perfect being. But all such proofs are ineffective, if what they aim at establishing is the actual existence of a being, arguing from concepts alone.

The situation is different, however, if the idea of God can be seen as a necessary posit of reason, which, in promulgating the idea, is 'occupied with nothing but itself' and its own full and consistent employment. (A, 680; B, 708.) While it does not assert dogmatically, 'Reality is a systematic whole', it does enjoin one to strive to order all empirical knowledge as if it formed such a whole. Thus it shows how 'we should *seek* to determine the constitution and connection of the objects of experience', not how objects really are constituted. (A, 671; B, 699.) To the extent that the programme is successful, the presupposition of an objective principle of systematic unity is vindicated; but the extent to which, and the conditions under which, it will succeed cannot be stated in advance. The ideas of reason possess 'objective but indeterminate validity'. (A, 663; B, 691.) Though partially vindicated, we do not know how closely, or in what ways nature conforms to them. For all we know they may grossly exaggerate the unity of things; and it may be objectively unnecessary (though it is necessary for human thought) to posit such models for a correct understanding of nature and its laws. So Kant summarises his doctrine by saying, 'We were not justified in assuming above nature a being with those qualities, but only in adopting the idea of such a being in order to view the appearances as systematically connected.' (A, 700; B, 728.)

5.4 THE REGULATIVE USE OF IDEAS

The concept of God, the necessary ground of all possibilities who is also the intelligent author of nature, is the concept of a being 'standing to the sum of appearances in a relation analogous to that in which appearances stand to one another'; specifically, as ground to consequent or cause to effect. (A, 674; B, 702.) But in removing all empirical conditions for applying the categories of causality, substance, reality, necessity and so forth we also remove all possibility of having any determinate concept whatsoever. We know that there cannot exist a transcendent being which is in itself as we conceive it to be. Yet we can construct the concept of such a being, by using the categories analogously; and, by doing so, we are able to see the empirical world in a particular light. The concept does not tell us supernatural facts; it presents the world to us under a certain aspect, namely, as a purposive, teleological, systematic unity. The idea of God 'decides nothing in regard to the ground of this unity or as to what may be the inner character of the being on which as cause the unity depends'. (A, 601.) It remains a model which is precluded from having a descriptive function, but which is necessary in its regulative use as a presupposition for aiming at the maximum systematic unity of natural laws.

It is important to see, however, that Kant does not regard the idea of God as *merely* regulative and immanent. He never wavers in his belief that there must be a transcendental 'ground of the order of the world' (A, 696; B, 724); since, by the doctrine of transcendental idealism, the world we know is only a sum of appearances, and cannot exist in itself as it appears to us. Though this ground must remain completely unknown to us, as it is in itself, it may and indeed must be thought of in terms of the analogical models provided by reason for the determination of the use of the understanding.

In the *Prolegomena*, Kant explains that the *Critique* set a boundary to human knowledge, in limiting the categories to the realm of phenomena. But a boundary, he says, belongs both to what is within and what is without it. So, in having knowledge of this boundary, reason may properly speak of 'the relation of that which lies outside the boundary to that which is contained inside it'. (P, 129; Ber. 4, 361.) It is, he claims, this *relation* which the ideas of reason depict, though they do so only relatively and analogically.

Ideas depict the relation of the transcendent to the world 'relatively, not absolutely'—the nature of the model is directed to the requirements of the subject and its faculties, not to an objective transcendent reality. (A, 676; B, 704.) Nevertheless, the model is a model of transcendent reality, conceived analogically, in terms of concepts which really only have meaning with reference to empirical reality. The question whether God in himself is like the model is meaningless; the idea is 'valid only in respect of the *employment* of our reason *in reference to the world*'. (A, 698; B, 726.) That is, it is will-directing and immanent; its function is to govern our acts in the world, and it is justified either as a condition of coherent investigation into nature, or as a condition of acceptance of the categorical demands of morality.

So it is misleading to ask 'does God exist?', as though that were a question of verifiable fact. We postulate the model of an author of nature 'solely for the purpose of penetrating to the innermost secrets of nature, in accordance with every possible principle of unity'. (A, 702; B, 730.) The schema of God helps us, as a regulative idea, to discover the greatest possible unity, order and purposiveness in the world. Though we must use that schema to see the world as a systematic unity, it must be a matter of complete indifference whether we say, 'God willed it so', or 'Nature arranged it so.' For we must conceive purposiveness as belonging to the essence of nature, not as imposed from without. The schema is only our way of conceiving the ground of nature, for the purposes of the employment of our cognitive faculties, and it must be denied any transcendent cognitive significance.

Kant's contention that the ideal of God is a postulate for the employment of understanding in the investigation of nature is not usually granted much force in contemporary thought.[3] The unity, order and necessity of natural laws are generally sought without any explicit recourse to the concept of an author of nature. But the analysis of theistic language which Kant elaborates provides the theoretical foundation for the doctrine of the postulates of practical reason, and makes clear their epistemological status.

Negatively, Kant's doctrine asserts that neither party to a dispute about the ultimate nature of reality has any speculative insight into the matter. Thus 'our practical interests . . . in a merely speculative dispute are never in any way affected'; for where we must admit speculative ignorance, our practical (moral) beliefs are unassailable and indisputable. (A, 744; B, 772.) Such notions as those of immortal souls or necessary beings cannot strictly be asserted as true, 'as we make no claims in regard to this

[3] Cf. P. F. Strawson, *The Bounds of Sense* (Methuen, London, 1966), 37.

latter domain' (of noumenal reality). (A, 769; B, 797.) But they can be used to guard the practical interests of reason, to secure moral faith 'against the misgivings which are apt to occur'. (A, 782; B, 810.) In this respect, they defend moral faith against speculative opinions which seem to undermine it, like dogmatic materialism; but they must be abandoned as soon as they have served that purpose. They give no knowledge whatsoever.

Positively, the absolute demands of categorical morality require the postulates of freedom, immortality and God as a condition of their intelligibility. These postulates function as models for that ground of the unity of nature and morality which must be presupposed if such a view of morality is to be tenable. The doctrine of language about the self and God which Kant sets out in the first *Critique* propounds the sense in which the postulates are to be understood and illustrates their centrality in Kant's thought. It is not too much to say that without this doctrine the theses of the primacy of practical reason and the categorical nature of moral obligation could not be maintained. Thus an appreciation of it is essential to a sympathetic understanding of Kant's ethical theory.

CHAPTER SIX

THE POSTULATES OF PRACTICAL REASON

6.1 THE SUMMUM BONUM

It was Heine who cynically suggested that Kant introduced the postulates of practical reason to comfort his manservant Lampe; and there has been a repeated tendency, in Kant criticism, to say that, as well as being based on very weak arguments, they are extraneous to and even incompatible with Kant's central stress on duty for its own sake. That Kant's specific arguments are weak is true; but then his specific arguments very often are weak. Yet his underlying insights continue to exert intellectual fascination and power. However, it must be admitted that even those commentators who are sympathetic to the doctrine of the categorical imperative, as set out in the *Groundwork,* and who might agree that the experience of duty is an inescapable fact of human life, often disavow those parts of Kant's arguments which speak of the *summum bonum* and of the necessary equation of virtue and happiness in an after-life, as being in conflict with his primary emphasis on the unconditionally binding character of obligation.

W. G. Maclagan puts this case particularly well when he writes, 'Suppose that man . . . were an emergent "accident" in a blind world-process'—suppose, that is, that there is most definitely no immortality and no supra-human intelligence, concerned for human happiness—yet 'the claim of the better, however exiguously better it be, is still to be heard; the "I ought" is as authoritative as ever it was.'[1] The view being proposed here is that I must take the moral law as supremely authoritative in my life, whatever my beliefs about the nature of the universe. Indeed, to do anything other than obey the moral law just because it is the moral law, whatever the facts, would be to fail to exhibit any

[1] W. G. Maclagan, *The Theological Frontier of Ethics* (Allen and Unwin, London, 1961), p. 60.

moral worth. For this reason, all thoughts of future happiness proportional to virtue must be positively excluded from consideration of one's duty; for such thoughts might well lead one to do right for the wrong motive—namely, out of hope of such future happiness. So it might well be argued, and often is, that Kant cannot introduce the doctrine of the *summum bonum* and the postulates of immortality and future happiness without threatening to undermine that supreme autonomy of the moral law which he stressed so much throughout his works. Sometimes, indeed, the doctrine of the *summum bonum* is completely ignored in expositions of Kant's ethics—as when Maritain writes, 'Kant . . . thought it was necessary to reject from morality as such the pursuit . . . of any good as the end of action, and especially the pursuit of the supreme good or of a supreme end.'[2] Kant is then interpreted as a pure formalist in ethics, who excluded any consideration of a supreme end or object of the human will, in favour of a theory asserting the purely formal criterion of moral judgment, that it must be universalisable, whatever its consequences.

This interpretation is plainly mistaken. Kant makes it quite clear in many places that his main concern in ethics is with human fulfilment and the happiness which is its natural corollary. The early formulations of this concern, in the form of the doctrine that happiness, together with the postulates which justify one in hoping for it, is the motive to morality have been discussed in sections 4.1–3. Though the terminology he then used of 'ground' and 'motive' was soon abandoned, the general doctrine remains and is elaborated in more detail in the Critical philosophy itself. It is, of course, true that Kant did stress, as no one had previously, the categorical nature of moral obligation, commitment to the moral law for its own sake. Yet what the formal principle of morality decrees, in its maxim of 'universal willing', is, as will be shown more fully in chapter seven, the pursuit of the richest development of one's powers consonant with the greatest possible social harmony.

Kant's view of morality is teleological, in that it sees obedience to the moral law as, at the same time, the fulfilment of human perfection. His objection to the rationalist ethics of Wolff was that one cannot *start* with an 'empty', non-moral, concept of

[2] J. Maritain, *Moral Philosophy* (Geoffrey Bles, London, 1964), p. 97.

G

metaphysical perfection and derive specific moral duties from it.
Nevertheless, starting from *a priori* laws of a pure will, the notion
of perfection can, he thought, be constructed as the ideal towards
which those laws point. Such a view is distinct from the view,
occasionally attributed to Kant, that the laws of duty are simply
obligatory in themselves, without reference to any end, or to
'perfection', as a harmonious system of ends. Obligatoriness is
connected intrinsically with an ideal of human perfection; and in
the same way the notion of human perfection is intrinsically connected with the notion of happiness. It is not the case that the
fulfilment of one's powers has no relevance to one's happiness.
Other things being equal, it is precisely in such fulfilment that
what Kant calls 'self-created' happiness is to be found. Perfection
is thus the mediating concept between 'duty' and 'happiness'; by
becoming perfect one attains self-wrought happiness; and perfection is defined, as an end, Kant thinks, by the moral law.
Commitment to implementing the moral law therefore implies
commitment to hope of the fulfilment of our whole nature as
persons, a fulfilment which will bring its own appropriate form of
happiness.

Kant states, 'The moral law . . . defines for us a final end, and
does so *a priori*, and makes it obligatory upon us to strive towards
its attainment. This end is the *summum bonum*.' (CTJ, 118; Ber.
5, 450.) He defines the *summum bonum* in this way: 'The highest
good means the whole, the perfect good, wherein virtue is always
the supreme good . . . while happiness . . . presupposes conduct in
accordance with the moral law as its condition.' (CPR, 115; Ber.
5, 110 f.) These are clear statements that there is a supreme end of
human action, which is determined *a priori* by the moral law;
and it may be defined as 'happiness in accordance with virtue'.

But what if this final end is impossible? It might be said that
the voice of duty would not be less absolute if the end which it
commanded was not possible; for Kant is quite clear that moral
laws 'are formal and command unconditionally, paying no regard
to ends (as the subject-matter of volition)'. (CTJ, 119; Ber. 5,
451.)

Thus Kant says that the only thing an atheist would have to
abandon would be 'the *premeditation* of the final end', not
obedience to the moral law. (CTJ, 119; Ber. 5, 451.) But, on the
other hand, he implies that the nullity of the final end would

weaken 'the respect with which he is immediately inspired to obedience' (CTJ, 121; Ber. 5, 452); which would in turn weaken the 'moral sentiment'. Further he writes, 'He must adopt the assumption [that the final end is possible] if he wishes to think in a manner consistent with morality.' (CTJ, 119; Ber. 5, 450.) It looks at times as though Kant both wants to have his cake and eat it. He wants to say that the postulate of a possible *summum bonum* is both necessary to the practice of morality and that it is not.

I think the reason for this difficulty is that Kant definitely wished to avoid making belief in God a *condition* of feeling moral obligation—this is part of the thesis of the autonomy of morals, for which he is justly famed. If this is so, it seems that the moral law must obligate, whether or not one believes that God exists. But what if one could *know* that God did not exist? Kant denies the logical possibility of making this move, because of the necessarily limited nature of human knowledge and the impossibility of theoretically establishing either the existence or non-existence of a future life or God.

Nevertheless, if we could, *per impossibile*, know the *summum bonum* to be impossible of attainment, obedience to the moral law for its own sake would become senseless and impossible. 'No man can possibly be righteous without having the hope . . . that righteousness must have its reward.' (LE, 54; Vor. 65.) Why should men obey this law, in a world in which no possibility of future happiness is held out, either to the individual after death or to the human race in some future time? One may indeed reply that such a question is quite out of order. The answer to the query, 'Why ought I to do my duty?' must simply be, 'Because it is my duty', otherwise one is attempting to reduce morality to prudence.

It is most important to notice that this attitude is just that which Kant himself characterises as 'misanthropical'. 'This misanthropic ethics', he says, 'sets moral conduct in opposition to all pleasures.' (LE, 77; Vor. 96.) Though such an ethics 'bases itself on man's pride and is productive of lofty deeds, and as such is good', yet 'it goes wrong . . . in holding that pleasure and morality are inconsistent with each other'. Though 'its morality is strict and precise', its 'hostility to pleasure is a mistake'. For 'to renounce happiness is to differentiate it from morality in a transcendental and unnatural way'. (LE, 78; Vor. 97.)

It is mistaken and misanthropical to deny a necessary relation of morality and happiness. While they are different in kind, they are both necessary elements of man's final good, and neither is complete without the other. 'Happiness is not a ground, not a principle of morality, but a necessary corollary of it.' (LE, 78; Vor. 97.) Thus the moral law does determine the will of itself; but it does so only as included in the concept of the *summum bonum*. If it was not included in that concept, as its supreme condition, it could not determine a rational will. Obedience to the moral law would be unintelligible.

It is interesting to note Kant's treatment of the situation envisaged by Maclagan. In the *Critique of Teleological Judgment*, Kant writes,

Let us ... take the case of a righteous man ... who considers himself firmly persuaded that there is no God and ... no future life either ... the end which this right-minded man would have, and ought to have, in view in his pursuit of the moral law, would certainly *have to be abandoned* by him as impossible. But perhaps he resolves to remain faithful to the call of his inner moral vocation ... if so, he must assume the existence of ... a God. (CTJ, 121; Ber. 5, 452.)

It is clear that Kant did not regard the notion of the *summum bonum* as an addendum to the doctrine of the categorical imperative, which did not affect that doctrine in any way. On the contrary, it is Kant's view that without the notion of the *summum bonum*, the doctrine of the categorical imperative would itself collapse as arbitrary, unintelligible and absurd.

6.2 THE RELATION OF HAPPINESS AND MORALITY

Though the moral law can only determine a rational will as part of the wider concept of the *summum bonum*, yet Kant stresses that it must be the law which determines the will; not the *summum bonum* as object of desire and not the thought of consequential happiness: 'Though the highest good may be the entire *object* of a ... pure will, it is still not to be taken as the *determining ground* of the pure will; the moral law alone must be seen as the ground for making the highest good and its realisation or promotion the object of the pure will.' (CPR, 113; Ber. 5, 109.) For the happiness which is part of the *summum bonum* is a specific sort of happiness, the desire for which must be awakened by the law itself, 'to which no selfish mind could have aspired'. (CPR, 135; Ber. 5, 130.)

Kant strongly criticises all those moral sense theorists who argue that moral action can be justified because it brings about a higher sort of happiness than that which comes from immoral or non-moral action. His criticism is on two main grounds. First, if one believed that one would be more happy by being more moral, then happiness *per se* would become the end of moral action. This, Kant thinks, would reduce morality to prudential self-interest—moral conduct would be for the sake of one's own greater happiness. And this is the proposition which the whole *Groundwork* so strongly contests.

Second, this distinction of higher and lower kinds of happiness in fact embodies a vicious circle. As he puts it, 'A man, if he is virtuous, will certainly not enjoy life without being conscious of his righteousness in each action . . . but can one make him virtuous . . . merely by commending to him the contentment of spirit which will arise from the consciousness of righteousness for which he as yet has no sense?' (CPR, 120; Ber. 5, 116.) That is, to say that a man will be happy only if he performs moral actions presupposes that one is talking about a moral man. It would not be true of a criminal, for instance, that he would actually be more happy performing moral acts; their performance would probably make him extremely miserable.

But, one may ask, would his performance of immoral acts not cause him to feel unhappy, by causing pangs of conscience? Such an objection, however, supposes that the man already has a conscience in good working order. Conscience is a thing which can very well be suppressed; and only the man who is virtuous will cultivate his conscience. Thus it may well be true that the happiness which derives from moral action is the greatest happiness, in some sense; but it can only be so for the man who is already moral. Therefore such happiness cannot be used as a motive to morality. The decision to act morally must be prior, logically and actually, to the judgment that a certain kind of happiness—moral happiness—is the best kind.

Now these points about happiness do not entail that happiness should not be part of the final object of man's willing, his final good. What they entail is that the object must not be happiness *per se*, of any quality; it must be happiness in accordance with morality. It is therefore impossible to perform moral acts for the sake of the future happiness which they bring. The nature of moral acts is that they are done for the sake of duty, and for no other reason. If they were done for the sake of happiness, they would not be moral, and consequently the happiness which can result only from moral action would not ensue. The end of human life is happiness; but if one acts for the sake of achieving happiness, one will be precluded from attaining it. It is only if one excludes happiness, as a ground of action, that it can be attained.

Kant holds, then, that the moral disposition must precede and be the condition of the desire for happiness: 'Morals has to do only with the rational condition of happiness and not with the means of achieving it.' (CPR, 135; Ber. 5, 130.) To make morality merely the means to happiness would be to espouse a 'coquettish' morality. Nevertheless, no account of morals can neglect happiness entirely without being unduly misanthropic.

Kant himself therefore locates his final doctrine between the two extremes of Stoicism and Epicureanism. The Stoics, he asserts, taught that 'whoever conducts himself well is happy' (LE, 7; Vor. 9); but in thus exalting virtue for its own sake, they deprive morality of a motive. The Epicureans, on the other hand, provide a motive—of happiness—but deprive it of all intrinsic worth. 'Both were at fault' (LE, 9; Vor. 11); for what is needed is a sort of happiness which can only be attained through intrinsically worthwhile action, realising intellectual and moral perfection. Kant comments in a similar vein on the Stoics, in the second *Critique*: 'They really left out of the highest good the second element [personal happiness], since they placed the highest good only in acting and in contentment with one's own personal worth . . . But the voice of their own nature could have sufficiently refuted this.' (CPR, 132; Ber. 5, 127.)

So Kant unequivocally asserts that the final end of happiness-in-accordance-with-virtue is 'imposed upon us by the law of duty', though it 'is not the foundation of duty'. (CTJ, 145; Ber. 5, 471.) And in the same place he asserts that, 'Could it [speculative reason] have perfect certainty as to the truth of this judgment, [that happiness will not be accorded to moral beings] it would have to look on the moral law itself as a mere delusion of our reason in respect of practical matters.' (*Loc. cit.*) So we must assume the possibility of the final end, 'in order not to fall into self-contradiction'.

If the *summum bonum* is impossible, 'the moral law which commands that it be furthered must be fantastic, directed to imaginary ends, and consequently inherently false'. Again, 'The impossibility of the highest good must prove the falsity of the moral law also.' (CPR, 118; Ber. 5, 114.) It is in this sense that 'dogmatic *unbelief* cannot stand side by side with a moral maxim'. (CTJ, 147; Ber. 5, 472.) These statements unmistakably declare Kant's belief that the possibility of the *summum bonum*, with all that implies, is a necessary condition of the intelligibility of the moral law and of what he terms 'the morality of intentions'.

6.3 THE UNION OF REASON AND SENSIBILITY

The hope for future happiness is necessary to moral action, in the sense that man's nature, as at once a moral and a sensuous being, a member of the phenomenal and the intelligible worlds, would be brought into contradiction with itself if such a hope were illusory. One would be forced to say that the fulfilment of the moral law was at the same time the denial of an important part of one's nature; such fulfilment would then be senseless, in that it would come to seem an arbitrary and unintelligible imposition of abstract reason upon man's sensuous being.

For Kant, if man consents to be determined to action by his desires, whatever they may be, then he is heteronomously determined; he abnegates his true character as a rationally determinable being. The legislation of the moral law which man himself creates is the true expression of man's autonomy and superiority over the sensuous bounds nature has set him. It is in such legislation that he begins to realise his transcendentally free nature and fulfil himself as a distinctively human person. The law of duty is thus known, practically, as supremely authoritative. All men, Kant holds, can come to know the obligatoriness of this law, in their own experience. For, in coming to know it, they are just coming to realise the full dignity of their own natures, as men. To realise his true humanity, man must act solely out of respect for this law of his own essential being.

But what if the law of autonomy is seen to contradict every
object or fulfilment of man's sensuous nature? What if it imposes
categorically upon every man the necessity of attaining absolute
moral worth; but this is completely without relation to happiness
or possible consequences? Why should the mere cultivation of
such an inner disposition be at all important? As Kant is reported
to have said in his *Lectures on Ethics*, 'Only God can see that our
dispositions are moral and pure, and if there were no God, why
ought we to cherish these dispositions?' (LE, 80; Vor. 100.)

He is not querying the fact that one intuitively perceives the
obligation to cultivate a holy will to be categorically imposed upon
one. But he is querying the validity of those intuitions themselves,
and suggesting the possibility that they may be delusory and
unreasonable. For what they obligate one to attain is a holy will—
something which in any case Kant holds to be finally unattainable
in this life, and something which concerns the inner disposition,
the personal worth of a man, rather than the nature of the world
which is to be affected by his moral acts. Indeed, it is Kant's
explicit doctrine that 'Even if . . . this will should wholly lack
power to accomplish its purpose . . . and there should remain only
the good will . . . like a jewel, it would still shine by its own light.'
(G, 11; Ber. 4, 394.) But the cultivation of such a disposition
could not be regarded as the law of our essential being if it contra-
dicted or ignored the demand of our sensuous nature for happiness; in this sense it would become absurd to cultivate it.

Kant always held that man is a being of both rationality and
sensibility. While it would be wrong to allow one's sensuous
impulses to govern one's reason—as Kant believed, with some
plausibility, that Hume maintained—the freedom and autonomy
of reason is not a freedom to contradict sensibility; it is a freedom
to order it in accordance with its own demands. The law of reason
in ethics, the moral law, is a purely formal principle, which
subjects the data of sensibility to itself, just as the laws of understanding in speculative knowledge, the categories, organise the
data of sensibility under purely formal principles, so as to make
knowledge of objects possible. In both cases the 'material' data of
sensibility must somehow be capable of being ordered by the
'formal' principles imposed upon them by the mind. In speculative knowledge, sensa must be capable of being ordered so as to
provide knowledge of a world of substances in reciprocal causal

relations. In ethics, the 'material' content of desires and impulses must be capable of being so ordered as to bring into being the Ideal of a world of rational beings united in the pursuit of a systematic harmony of purposes.

The doctrine of the two distinct but necessarily related elements of the *summum bonum*—virtue and happiness—should be seen as just a particular case of the general Critical standpoint that man is a member of two worlds, the sensible and the intelligible, and that it is his vocation to subsume the data of sensibility under the demands of reason. But if, in ethics, such a subsumption should turn out to be impossible—if reason can only contradict the essential end of our sensuous nature, happiness— then the human person disintegrates into two conflicting parts. We cannot make happiness our goal, because reason always reminds us of the demands of morality. And we cannot make the pursuit of virtue alone our goal, because the voice of our own sensuous nature condemns such an ideal as futile and impossible.

In some way Kant needs to reconcile the two assertions, 'as far as our nature as sensible beings is concerned, our happiness is the only thing of importance' (CPR, 63; Ber. 5, 61); and, 'the majesty of duty has nothing to do with the enjoyment of life'. (CPR, 91; Ber. 5, 88.) Both of these assertions are true, but they leave a marked tension within human nature which moralists have been prone to resolve by opting for one side of human nature at the expense of the other. In Kant's view, an adequate account of human morality must take full and equal account of both aspects.

This can be done, he thinks, because in the end the whole phenomenal world is just an appearance of intelligible reality, and in moral commitment man regards himself as part of that reality: 'The person as belonging to the world of sense is subject to his own personality, so far as he belongs to the intelligible world.' (CPR, 89; Ber. 5, 87.) Kant's language about this doctrine may well seem to be self-contradictory. On the one hand he writes that the idea of 'a nature in which reason would bring forth the highest good were it accompanied by sufficient physical capacities . . . really stands as a model for the determination of our will'; and then only with regard to one's maxims, not to its possible effects in the world. (CPR, 45; Ber. 5, 43.) Again, the category of 'causality' which the moral law leads one to postulate

'is exclusively practical, since the idea of the law of causality . . .
has causality itself or is its determining ground'. (CPR, 51; Ber. 5,
50.) Such passages as these suggest that the notion of an intelligible realm has no cognitive significance whatsoever; that it is
only the *idea* of it which is believed to determine the will to act in
a specific way; that it is a heuristic fiction.

On the other hand Kant writes that the intelligible world 'has
under it the entire world of sense, including the empirically
determinable existence of man in time', which suggests that some
cognitive significance must be given to the concept of an
intelligible realm. (CPR, 89; Ber. 5, 86.) Not surprisingly,
commentators have been apt to take one of these interpretations
to the exclusion of the other. It is here that Kant's doctrine of
theistic language, sketched in section 5.4, helps one to see how
both views can be held without self-contradiction.

That there must be an intelligible ground of appearances is not
in doubt. But the concepts one uses to think of it have an
exclusively 'practical', will-determining use. The way in which
we thus conceive the possibility of moral action, as free conformity to the general will of a community of rational spirits, is
purely subjective; a condition of human reason, not of things-in-
themselves. Intelligible reality may not in itself take the form of
such a community of persons; but we must conceive it as we do
if the categorical nature of moral obligation is to be reasonably
maintained.

When it is appreciated that intelligibly free action must be
regarded as the real ground of nature for Kant, it can be seen how
the conception of morality as realising the demands of reason
necessarily entails the harmonisation of virtue—the formal
characteristic of all rational willing—with happiness—man's
contentment as a sensuous being, determined by the moral law.

In the world of appearance, it seems that man is determined by
nature and is dependent upon it for his weal or woe. But moral
commitment licenses one to postulate a real intelligible ground of
nature itself, and further to suppose that, in one's moral decisions,
or at least one's ultimate noumenal moral decision, one is oneself
determinative of nature in its phenomenal aspects.

The position of the Critical philosophy of ethics, then, is that
man, *qua* legislative practical reason, must be regarded as a real
determining ground of nature, otherwise the moral law, which

reason promulgates, loses its possibility and *a fortiori* its binding force. And if reason must be conceived as determining nature, it must be conceived as determining the world to a condition of happiness in accordance with virtue; for the moral law must be regarded as the law of the fulfilment of man's whole nature, sensuous as well as intelligible. This postulate is already involved in taking morality to be a matter of categorical obligations imposed by reason.

6.4 THE TELEOLOGICAL NATURE OF KANTIAN ETHICS

One aim in sketching the development of the widely-known ethical views of the *Groundwork* has been to counter the idea that Kant is purely a Stoic philosopher of stern duty by placing his ethical doctrines in their wider context of a spiritual and purposive view of reality. Indeed, if religion is understood to consist in metaphysical beliefs about God, the soul and immortality, rather than in specific cults or practices, Kant's ethics is essentially religious.

I have tried to substantiate the claim that if this general spiritual view was abandoned the Kantian notion of 'duty' would have to be abandoned also as irrational and unintelligible. The point must, I think, be stressed, in an academic tradition which tends to learn little of Kant's ethics beyond the doctrine of the categorical imperative, and which therefore sometimes castigates it as expressing simply an irrational, even pathological, reliance on a bare 'sense of duty'. It is sometimes said that the Kantian 'sense of duty' has no necessary relation to actual human purposes or desires, or to what makes for human flourishing and happiness. So it comes to seem at best an austere and puritanical doctrine, and at worst a pointless, silly and dangerously authoritarian one.

Such interpretations can only arise through ignorance. While Kant held that moral effort is of supreme worth, and while he believed that particular duties were somehow derivable from a purely formal principle, he always held that the pursuit of morality would be senseless if it was not aimed at the realisation of one's natural perfections in a harmonious community. His main ethical concern was with human fulfilment and the conditions of its attainment. In the following chapter, I intend to show that this is true even of the *Groundwork*, the concern of

which with the formulation of one supreme formal principle of
morality has perhaps misled many critics. And I shall trace the
final development of the metaphysical or religious doctrines which
Kant saw as necessary to make the pursuit of perfection rational,
given that human fulfilment is unattainable in this world.

There are two questions which may be raised against the
interpretation of Kant I am proposing. First, is it not the case
that Kant's ethical system is well able to survive the abandonment
of its metaphysical context, however true it may be to say that it
originated in such a context? One can, for instance, construct a
purely descriptive account of the logic of moral discourse,
bringing out perhaps the features of universalisability, impartiality and autonomy which it contains and the substantive rule of
respect for persons which it embodies, rather as R. M. Hare and
R. S. Downie[3] have done. Or one could go further and attempt
to justify or 'transcendentally deduce' the general features of
moral discourse by consideration of the nature of man as a
rational being affected by desires. In both cases, it may be said,
there is a recognisably Kantian theory of ethics, without any
appeal to religious or transcendent metaphysics. And such views,
it may further be argued, represent a proper development of
Kant's Critical philosophy towards a full acceptance of metaphysics as 'immanent', or as concerned solely with *a priori*
features of experience, or perhaps with necessary conditions of
our linguistic scheme. The religious beliefs, it may be said, were
never integral to his theory, and their presence even renders it
uncomfortably inconsistent.

It is certainly true that such views can be developed from and
are expressed in Kant's writings on ethics. But even if one were
convinced that they are all that can be salvaged of his ethical
views for contemporary use, it is equally certain that they do not
give the whole Kantian story, and even that they omit consideration of what was most central to Kant's ethical concern, the
notion of human flourishing. Even the basic doctrine of the categorical imperative needs to be put in the context of a wider concern with the fulfilment of human and natural purposes before it
can be fairly interpreted. Though Kant often expressed the

[3] Cf. R. M. Hare, *The Language of Morals* (Oxford University Press,
1952), and R. S. Downie and E. Telfer, *Respect for Persons* (Allen and
Unwin, London, 1969).

doctrine of religion in such a way that it could appear superfluous to his central tenets—though, that is, he expressed himself badly —a study of the development of his thought leads irresistibly to the conclusion that the religious concern was always paramount for Kant himself.

An intelligible ethical theory can certainly be extracted from the Kantian metaphysical context. Indeed, his doctrine is so complex that a number of alternative methods of demythologisation present themselves, depending largely upon the interests of the interpreter. But if one is concerned to ask what the topics were with which Kant most frequently concerned himself, throughout the course of his life, I do not think there can be any doubt that the doctrine of human perfection, and the conditions of its possibility, would take pride of place. Kant did not give up the religious context of his ethical thought, even when the methodological axioms of the Critical philosophy clearly made a religious view difficult for him to defend. And I think it would be a misinterpretation to see the postulates as redundant additions to an already complete theory. Rather, they are concepts which help to define Kant's whole view of ethics; even though, for various reasons, he does not finally succeed in formulating satisfactorily the intrinsic connexion he always sought between morals and metaphysical belief. So I do not think that Kantian ethical theory can survive the abandonment of its metaphysical context, without undergoing a transformation which would eliminate Kant's central concerns.

The second question which could be raised against this interpretation is whether Kant did not come to see that morals must be divorced from all speculative questions of metaphysics whatsoever, in his doctrine of the primacy of practical reason. Though in the *Groundwork* he toyed with the idea of founding moral freedom on speculatively established spontaneity, he abandoned this view in the second *Critique*, and held that morality must be completely self-justifying, and could, indeed, outweigh any speculative conclusions in cases of conflict. Does this not suggest a complete divorce of morality from metaphysical speculation?

It is true that Kant upheld the primacy of practical reason; but it must be remembered that any account of morality in terms of practical reason is itself necessarily speculative. So one cannot interpret the doctrine of the primacy of practical reason in such a way as to make it logically prior to any speculative thinking whatever. The force of the doctrine must be, as indeed Kant says it is (cf. CPR, 124–6; Ber. 5, 119–24), that speculative reason cannot positively deny propositions which it is not able to establish, but which remain empty possibilities until postulated by practical reason. It is therefore clear that Kant did not believe that moral considerations could be quite divorced from speculative concerns. Speculation is not needed for us to come to know the moral law and its absolute obligatoriness. But this does not mean that there are no metaphysical presuppositions or implications of our knowledge of absolute obligation. Metaphysical analysis is necessary, not for knowledge of what one ought to do, but for uncovering the conditions of the possibility of the synthetic *a priori* propositions of morality and tracing them to their source in the activity of practical reason. Kant's claim is simply that moral experience, once speculatively construed in this specific way, can of itself give rise to further postulates which reason must then integrate within its general conceptual structure and not merely reject as not being subject to empirical verification. Far from the doctrine of the primacy of practical reason effecting a complete divorce between theory and practice, it gives rise to what Kant explicitly calls new 'theoretical positions' which are not grounded in sense-experience. But one may further say that Kant underestimates or ignores the extent to which his view of morality as consisting in necessary laws aiming at human perfection depends on a wider, purely speculative view of the nature of reason and its place in nature. This wider view, with its origins in rationalism and Pietistic Christianity, is clear in Kant's pre-Critical writings; it is preserved in the Critical doctrine of the postulates; and it is fully developed in his later writings. One main purpose of this book is to make this view clear, and to show its centrality for an adequate understanding of Kant's view of ethics.

CHAPTER SEVEN

THE SUPREME PRINCIPLE OF MORALITY

7.1 THE DERIVATION OF DUTIES FROM THE CATEGORICAL IMPERATIVE

It would be quite impossible to include commentaries on the *Groundwork*, the second *Critique* and the *Metaphysic of Morals* in one book, much less this one, the primary concern of which is with the wider context of Kant's thought into which these central ethical writings fit. In any case, excellent commentaries already exist on the central ethical works, which I have listed in the Bibliography. But it is probably worthwhile to show how the general interpretation which I am suggesting bears on the more familiar texts. Accordingly, I shall examine two of the main issues raised in these works, the nature of the supreme principle of morality and the application of the principle to provide specific duties. And I shall try to show, in each case, how the interpretation of Kant's ethics in teleological terms not only illuminates, but is necessary to render intelligible, Kant's treatment of these issues.

The *Groundwork* is explicitly concerned with the formulation of the supreme principle of morality. All commentators are agreed that this principle is expressed in the first formula of the categorical imperative: 'Act only on that maxim whereby thou canst at the same time will that it should become a universal law.' (G, 46; Ber. 4, 421.) But Kant proceeds to discuss four other formulae of the same principle; and commentators do not agree either on the relation of these formulae to each other, or on what exactly Kant means by a 'supreme principle of morality'. In addition, there are two further important formulae which Kant produces in the *Metaphysic of Morals*; the formula of juridical duty: 'act externally in such a manner that the free exercise of thy will may be able to coexist with the freedom of all others, according to a universal law' (MEJ, 46; Ber. 6, 231); and the formula of duties of virtue: 'act according to a maxim of *ends* which it can be a universal law for everyone to have'. (MM, 55; Ber. 6, 395.) These must also be taken into account in any adequate discussion of Kant's doctrine.

I have shown how Kant developed the doctrine of one supreme formal principle of morality with the aid of Rousseau's doctrine of the general will and Swedenborg's notion of an intelligible world, and in parallel with his development of the concept of the speculative intellect as promulgating purely formal *a priori* principles which are applicable to the phenomenal world. And I have also shown how basic underlying themes of Kant's ethical thinking are, first, a concern for the happiness and perfection of all rational beings, and second, a belief in the infinite and intrinsic worth of the will which acts from motives of duty. These themes may well reflect the influence on Kant of rationalism and Pietism, respectively. They certainly complicate the question of the place of the categorical imperative in Kant's ethics. And their development from Kant's earliest writings undermines such views as those of A. R. C. Duncan,[1] who holds that the subsidiary formulae of the categorical imperative were taken from Christian Garve's 1783 translation and commentary on Cicero's *De Officiis*, and that they mistakenly led Kant to deviate from his main purpose in an attempt to show that his *a priori* principle could give rise to particular duties (cf. Duncan, pp. 175 ff.). While it is indisputable that Kant was influenced by the Stoic conceptions of the law of nature, the universal human society and the intrinsic dignity of man, the sources for the various formulae of the categorical imperative are much more various than that, and they enter basically and importantly into the development of his Critical view, not just as interludes or deviations from his 'main theme' of providing a definition of what morality is.

The various formulations of the categorical imperative all have a significant part to play in the derivation of particular duties. But though all commentators are agreed that Kant does attempt to derive particular duties from the supreme principle of morality, they do not agree on the centrality of such derivation to Kant's purpose in writing the *Groundwork*, or on the way in which they are to be derived, or on the significance of the different formulae

---

[1] A. R. C. Duncan, *Practical Reason and Morality* (Nelson, London, 1957).

he provides. I shall hold that such derivation is central to Kant's aims; I shall illustrate the rather complex way in which Kant goes about such derivation; and I shall hold that the different formulae are significantly different in import, even though Kant, at one point, maintains that 'the three modes of presenting the principle of morality . . . are at bottom only so many formulae of the very same law, and each of itself involves the other two'. (G, 65; Ber. 4, 436.)

The starting-point for discussion of this issue is quite naturally to be found in Kant's statement that principles of action are prohibited morally if they could not be universalised without contradiction, or if they could not be willed as universal laws (cf. G, 49; Ber. 4, 424). Some critics have interpreted this, rather curiously, to mean that in every situation there is one and only one principle of action which could be willed as a universal law. The principles which are possible are limited by the facts of the situation, including, presumably, facts about the agent's character and desires. But then it is alleged that in every situation there is only one principle which a rational agent could will everyone relevantly similar to him in relevantly similar circumstances to follow. At least this interpretation is more sensible than one which tries to deduce duties from the supreme principle by itself, in abstraction from all particular contexts or anticipated consequences of action. But it seems clear that this view is not Kant's, and would have been condemned by him as exemplifying 'fantastic virtue', which 'admits nothing morally indifferent and strews all [man's] steps with duties, as with man-traps'. (MM, 71; Ber. 6, 409.) Many of our everyday actions are morally indifferent or permissible, not positively obligatory.

What one must say is that not every universalisable act is a duty; but every act which is not universalisable is morally prohibited. Thus, in any particular situation, a man should never act on a principle which would contradict itself, if made a universal law. The categorical imperative can be used to inform one what is morally prohibited; and this will, of course, often enjoin duties. If, for instance, breaking a promise is morally prohibited, it follows that keeping the promise is morally obligatory, since these are contradictory principles. On the other hand, if lying is prohibited, it will not immediately follow that telling the truth is obligatory; since here one often has the alternative of saying

H

nothing. So the categorical imperative, on this interpretation, will only enjoin those duties which are the contradictories of actions on prohibited principles.

Most commentators are agreed that this criterion is not success-ful in yielding specific moral duties, though Singer has defended it at some length.[2] But few of them have seen how Kant meant to apply it. For they have tended to confine their attention to the *Groundwork* derivation of four typical duties: preservation of life (a perfect duty to oneself); promise-keeping (a perfect duty to others); self-realisation (an imperfect duty to oneself) and beneficence (an imperfect duty to others) (cf. G, 47 ff., 56 ff.; Ber. 4, 421 ff., 429 f.). But these short sections merely prefigure the full derivation of particular duties from the supreme prin-ciple of morality, which is systematically undertaken in the *Metaphysic of Morals*. It is that work which makes clear the centrality of Kant's concern with the derivation of specific duties from the supreme principle.

He divides the *Metaphysic of Morals* into two main parts, the 'Doctrine of Law' and the 'Doctrine of Virtue'. In the former, Kant is concerned only with what he terms 'juridical duties', duties which can be legally enforced, and which restrict the pur-suit of one's chosen ends in ways which allow a like liberty to all other citizens. Such duties make no reference to men's motives for action, but are solely concerned with the external rightness of acts—that is, their compatibility with a similar freedom of action for all men. And they are not concerned with men's purposes in acting; they give each man a freedom to pursue whatever purposes he wishes, as long as those purposes do not interfere with the similar purposes of others. Juridical duties are thus prohibitive or limiting duties, which simply restrict one's actions so as to allow the maximum possible external freedom that every-one, in an antecedent position of choice, could agree to. As Kant puts it, 'The maxims of actions can be *arbitrary*, and come only under . . . the limiting condition that they qualify for giving universal law.' (MM, 49; Ber. 6, 389.) So far, almost any action could be willed universally, for any purpose, and with any motive. All the categorical imperative would exclude would be partiality, or making an exception in one's own case. As long as one's maxims leave an equal freedom for all to will the same way, one is

[2] M. Singer, *Generalisation in Ethics* (Knopf, New York, 1961).

allowed to will even the subordination of one's person to inclination.

The second part of the *Metaphysic of Morals*, however, dramatically enlarges this negative, limiting use of the categorical imperative. Duties of virtue, Kant holds, are concerned, not with outer freedom, but with 'inner freedom', freedom from inclination, to pursue the rational ends of one's nature, in the fullest use of one's free powers. Such duties cannot be legally enforced, since they are primarily concerned with the purposes one has in acting, and with the motives from which one acts. They do not enjoin specific actions, like juridical duties, but only maxims for actions, or purposes which may be expressed in many different acts. Whereas juridical laws simply limit the permissible means to the purposes one happens to have, whatever they are, ethical laws enjoin the pursuit of particular purposes, 'ends which are also duties'. And the motive for pursuing such purposes must be simply that of dutifulness for its own sake, since no legal sanctions can apply to the free adoption of purposes. Kant writes that if there were no ends which were also duties, which are necessarily furthered by reason, 'a *categorical* imperative would be impossible', since all purposes would then have to be taken from inclination. (MM, 43; Ber. 6, 385.)

What, then, are these morally obligatory purposes, and how are they established? From the principle that what '*can* be an end, that *is* an end for pure practical reason', Kant defines the ends which are also duties as those purposes which one could will everyone to have (or, perhaps more strictly, which one could not will everyone to lack). (MM, 56; Ber. 6, 395.) He now provides the new formula of the categorical imperative: 'Act according to a maxim of *ends* which it can be a universal law for everyone to have.' (*Loc. cit.*) It is regrettable that what is probably the least misleading formulation of the fundamental principle of ethics, since it refers explicitly to human purposes, never appears in the work devoted to elucidating that principle.

But though Kant clearly maintains that ethics must speak of purposes, and so must refer to the empirically given purposes which men, considered in their general character as rational animals, do have; he still holds that the purposes of moral action are to be defined by the purely formal concept of the moral law, limiting the pursuit of some purposes and enjoining the pursuit

of others as obligatory. 'If . . . we try to determine duties by
beginning with . . . the *end*, rather than with the form of the will,
the *law* . . . then we shall indeed have no *metaphysical first
principles* of the doctrine of virtue.' (MM, 33; Ber. 6, 376 f.) The
obligatory purposes, which one could not rationally will all men
to lack, Kant places under the two headings of happiness and
perfection, the two necessary elements of the *summum bonum*.
Rational agents necessarily will that all sensuous beings should
aim at happiness, in so far as this is not incompatible with the
happiness of others. And they necessarily will that their physical
and intellectual powers (which enable them to prescribe and
realise all sorts of purposes) and their freedom from sensuous
inclinations (which enables them to act for the sake of duty alone)
should be developed and perfected.

In elaborating these necessary purposes of reason, Kant begins
by considering duties to oneself, which he believes to be the
foundation of all duties. He divides them into two main classes,
perfect duties and imperfect duties to oneself. There are compli-
cations about this definition which cannot be considered here;
and I shall say, in a summary way, that perfect duties to oneself
are 'duties of virtue' rather than of law, because one cannot be
externally compelled to obey them, by legal sanctions. But they
are 'perfect' duties, in the sense that they allow no exceptions in
the interests of inclination. They are limiting, negative, duties,
which *'forbid* man to act contrary to the end of his nature'. (MM,
82; Ber. 6, 419.) Imperfect duties to oneself allow a certain
latitude, in that they may occasionally be ignored, and they do not
specify the number of times one should perform such duties, or
the way in which, or extent to which, one should perform them.
For instance, one has an imperfect duty to be beneficent; but
that does not specify how often, how greatly, or in what way one
should show one's beneficence; and one may, on particular
occasions, do less than would be absolutely possible, without
incurring moral blame. Unfortunately, the *Groundwork* and the
Metaphysic of Morals have different definitions of imperfect
duties. Whereas in the *Groundwork*, an imperfect duty is said to
allow exceptions from duty in the interests of inclination, in the
Metaphysic of Morals this is denied, and the only permissible
exceptions are said to arise when duties conflict. (G, 46; Ber. 4,
421. MM, 49; Ber. 6, 390.) Still, one may partially reconcile the

conflict by saying that one can never be exempted from having the general purpose of beneficence, for instance; but one is allowed a certain latitude in deciding how and when to implement this purpose. Imperfect duties are what Kant calls 'widening' positive duties, which '*command* [man] to make a certain object of choice his end'. (MM, 82; Ber. 6, 419.) The prohibitive duties aim at 'the *preservation* of his nature in its perfection'; while the positive duties 'concern his *perfecting* of himself', and lead man to develop the power to realise all his purposes and make himself more perfect than nature made him.

Although happiness is, for Kant, a necessary aim of human action, it is not a duty to seek one's own happiness, since every man seeks his own happiness by nature in any case, and so does not have to be constrained to do so. It is, however, a duty to aim at the happiness of others, by refraining from interfering with their permissible purposes and by helping them to achieve them, in general. Moreover, Kant argues that it is impossible to aim at the perfection of others, though of course one can help others in their self-chosen pursuit of perfection, since it is logically impossible to prescribe a purpose for another person. Thus duties to others are duties of love and respect (helping them to achieve their aims, while never regarding them simply as a means to the furtherance of one's own aims); and duties to oneself are perfect duties of preserving one's natural and moral capacities and imperfect duties of cultivating one's physical and mental powers, and one's ability freely to control the wayward powers of the desires.

It is clear that Kant takes it to be obvious that there are ends of human nature which ought to be preserved and perfected. He divides these ends into two classes, the ends of animal nature and the ends of purely moral nature. The former are 'impulses of nature having to do with man's *animality*'—namely, instincts aiming at self-preservation, the preservation of the species and preservation of one's powers of enjoyment. The latter consists in 'the *dignity* of humanity', by which man, as a morally free agent, is superior to all desires and inclinations. This dignity, Kant believes, must be preserved in the face of all temptations to become simply 'a plaything of the mere inclinations', to sit loosely to one's principles when they become unpleasant or difficult to uphold.

It appears that it is nature which sets before man ends which, negatively, may not be violated, and positively, need to be furthered by personal effort. Reason must preserve and perfect the purposes of nature; and it must ultimately transcend those purposes, in realising its own infinite value in free commitment to moral action. Kant thought that by consideration of the purposes which men do have according to natural laws, which they could will to be universal, one could arrive at a doctrine of the ends men ought to have, which must be either preserved from violation or perfected. And he regards these ends as very largely set by nature, which he assumes to be teleologically constituted, so that the existence of such 'natural ends' sets limits to what men are able spontaneously to choose as particular purposes. He writes, 'By reason of the ends which all men naturally have it is easy to state what one's duty is.' (MM, 32; Ber. 6, 375.) Since the ends which men 'naturally have' are ends set by nature and not autonomously chosen, Kant conceives that reason and nature are positively related, and that reason must take account of and seek to perfect the purposes of nature. In doing so, it freely determines nature in accordance with nature's own inner purposes.

This expresses an unmistakable echo of the Stoic view that virtue consists of a will which is in agreement with the ends of nature, or 'in harmony with nature'. On the one hand, one is forbidden to act contrary to the ends of one's nature; and on the other hand, one is enjoined to perfect one's nature and power to realise all possible ends. With regard to these positive duties, the moral law leaves it open exactly what one should do, or how far one should pursue these obligatory ends. Ethics simply states 'the system of the ends of pure practical reason', and leaves scope for human judgment and decision, in implementing them. (MM, 39; Ber. 6, 381.)

Even in the *Groundwork*, which has often been interpreted as expounding a purely formal principle of universality, without any regard to purposes or consequences, it is difficult to fail to see Kant's underlying view of morality as a system of the laws of 'universal practical reason', aimed at realising the ideal of a Kingdom in which 'all ends [are] combined in a systematic whole'. (G, 62; Ber. 4, 433.) And in the *Metaphysic of Morals*, it is made quite explicit that legislative reason promulgates, not a senseless set of absolute imperatives, but the rational condition of a harmonious system of ends, the greatest possible realisation of individual purposes and the greatest possible harmony of all human purposes which are compatible with, and yet transcend through spontaneous volition, the purposes of nature.

7.2 REASON AND THE ENDS OF NATURE

Kant's own method of deriving specific duties from the supreme principle of morality is very different from that attempted by many Kant critics, who have tried to suggest that morally prohibited acts are those which are logically self-contradictory, when made universal. It is an essential part of his method to refer to purposes of nature which a rational agent who is part of nature cannot will to contravene or neglect, without 'contradicting', in a non-logical sense, his own nature as a rational and sensuous being. This is brought out in the second *Groundwork* formulation of the categorical imperative ('Act as if the maxim of thy action were to become by thy will a universal law of nature'; G, 46; Ber. 4, 421) and in the 'Typic of Pure Practical Reason' (CPR, 70 ff.; Ber. 5, 67 ff.), when Kant proposes that one should ask whether one's maxim in acting could be willed as a universal law of nature. As Paton has pointed out (cf. *The Categorical Imperative*, ch. 15), this proposal presupposes a purposive understanding of nature, so that one is to ask what natural purposes one would create in the world, if one had the power. If it happens that the natural purposes of nature are just those that I would rationally choose, then I am bound not to frustrate those natural ends merely for the sake of inclination.

Kant applies this principle in his treatment of suicide, in the *Groundwork*. (G, 47; Ber. 4, 421 f.) He argues that the maxim, 'If life offers nothing but misery, I will die' could not be a universal law of nature. For the maxim is founded on 'self-love'; and a system of nature in which self-love, the function of which is to improve life, also destroyed life, 'would contradict itself', and could not exist as a system of nature. The claim is that one could not both will the existence of self-love as a purpose of nature, and also the frustration of that purpose by allowing the feeling to contradict its proper purpose.

The argument is both obscure and confused. It is not at all clear that one would ever commit suicide from 'self-love', especially if self-love comprises a certain contentment and fulfilment of inclination. One might take one's life to avoid pain or misery, but the avoidance of pain is not equivalent to the pursuit of pleasure; and both are distinct from the instinct for self-preservation which is the nearest a Darwinian could get to a 'purpose of nature' in this respect. Even if there is 'a feeling whose special nature it is to impel to the improvement of life', there is no reason why it should be this same feeling which leads one to commit suicide, and no reason why it should not be over-ruled by some other feeling, whose special nature it is to impel one to avoid misery, in appropriate circumstances.

To allow Kant still more rope, there is no reason why self-love should not permit one to commit suicide when no prospect of further improvement is apparent. For such a feeling to lead to one end in most situations, and a contradictory end in totally different circumstances, far from being self-contradictory, seems totally reasonable. Kant's argument would be plausible if the proposed maxim was: 'Even when life offers prospects for improvement, I will kill myself'; and one proposed to do this with the motive of self-love; and self-love had the natural purpose of impelling to the improvement of life. But it loses all force when life offers no prospects for improvement (i.e. when the situation alters radically); when I do not propose to kill myself from the motive of self-love (but from, say, boredom with life or fear of pain); or when one does not concede that nature has purposes which one must take account of, and not contravene.

A similar emphasis on purposes of nature is found in the derivation of the perfect duties which absolutely forbid masturbation, gluttony and drunkenness. Kant states that 'the natural function of sexual love is to preserve the species'; so to frustrate 'nature's purpose' for the sake of pleasure is prohibited. (MM, 87; Ber. 6, 424.) The ground of proof, he says, is that, in using sex simply as a means to pleasure, one completely abandons oneself to animal inclination, and so uses one's personality merely as a means to pleasure. The appeal here is not to what one could will for all beings like oneself; nor has it got anything to do with frustrating or refusing to realise some purpose which one has freely set oneself, and which could be similarly pursued by all men. What is being said is that the adoption of some purposes—like gratification through masturbation—is prohibited, because they contravene purposes of nature and they subordinate one's human dignity to 'animal inclination'. In the *Padagogik* Kant mistakenly asserts that masturbation leads to sterility and early senility, and to this extent it is akin to gluttony, which incapacitates one for skilful or deliberative actions. (Ber. 9, 497.) There thus seem to be three sorts of argument hinted at here—that such purposes are misuses of the purposes of nature (sex preserves the species and eating preserves the individual); they frustrate the ability to use one's powers purposefully; and they degrade man to the level of an animal. The two latter arguments will be dealt with in section 7.4. But the appeal to purposes of nature is repeated by Kant in the derivation of the duties of truth-telling (where lying is said to be 'opposed to the natural purposiveness of the power of communicating one's thoughts'); self-realisation (which develops 'the capacities of greater perfection, which belong to the end that nature has in view in regard to humanity in ourselves'); and beneficence (where Kant writes that men are 'united by nature in one dwelling place for the purpose of helping one another'). (MM, 93; Ber. 6, 429. G, 58; Ber. 4, 430. MM, 121; Ber. 6, 453.)

It may seem as though Kant's talk of purposes of nature is quite incompatible with his insistence, in the *Groundwork*, that morality must be autonomous. By this he means, at least in part, that moral laws must spring from one's own will; for he thinks that if they were objective, in the sense of being founded on some reality independent of the human will, they would only be binding hypothetically, on condition that one desired to obey them. If morality is the law of one's own will, however, one is necessarily bound to obey it, as the law of one's essential being, apart from any contingent desires one may have.

Nevertheless, practical reason must take account of particular purposes, since 'pure practical reason is a power of ends as such, and for it to be indifferent to ends or to take no interest in them would be a contradiction'. (MM, 56; Ber. 6, 395.) When the categorical imperative is to be applied, one must consider the nature of man in general and as such. Now Kant considers that everything in nature has a purpose (cf. G, 12; Ber. 4, 395); and so knowledge of the nature of man will include knowledge of the essential purposes of the human faculties, the purposes which make human nature what it is. So when practical reason considers what purposes it can legislate as obligatory, in accordance with the formal principle of universality, for men as such, the purposes will be just those which are intrinsically involved in human nature, which can be preserved and developed by human action. This procedure is not heteronomous, for it does not begin from a definition of human perfection, defined antecedently to any morality, which is then alleged to be objectively binding on the human will. Rather, it begins with the human will, and defines human perfection in terms of what one can legislate universally for beings of a specifically human nature. It is not because something is a purpose of nature that it is obligatory—to say that would be to espouse heteronomy. Nature's purposes become obligatory ends because one necessarily legislates their preservation by all rational animals; and it is one's autonomous willing that stipulates that the purposes of nature shall constitute 'perfection', and binds one to pursue them as fully as possible: 'The moral law is that which first defines the concept of the good.' (CPR, 66; Ber. 5, 64.)

Now one can say that, given the knowledge that man is a sensuous rational being, one can see that it is his function, *qua* sensuous being, to pursue happiness, and, *qua* rational being, to pursue all possible purposes, in independence of desire. It is at this point, after the teleological concept of nature has done its work, that the categorical imperative comes into play and decrees the preservation and perfecting of the 'essential ends of humanity'. The neglect of these ends could not be willed by a rational being, in the sense that thereby such a being would deny its very purpose in existing, its essential nature.

One can now see why Kant thinks that one could not will all rational beings to commit suicide, out of fear of pain. Such an act would destroy all one's mental and moral powers, one's capacities for rational action; and it would subordinate one's rational nature to the pressure of mere inclinations. Accordingly, it could simply not be willed by a being whose very nature was to achieve independence of inclinations. The appeal to universalisability is not directly relevant, in the case of duties to oneself, except as a means for getting one to adopt an impartial attitude to one's own situation. For the purposes which one could not rationally will all men to lack are just those purposes which are essential to each individual, as a sensuous rational being. It seems that the basic moral principle involved here is not simply that of universalisability, but the principle that a rational being should not contradict its essential ends, or subordinate its supreme dignity to any contingent desires. For to do that would be to diminish human nature; and this would be a sort of 'internal inconsistency' in the will.

Although it is quite clear that Kant's account relies heavily on a purposive understanding of human nature, Mary Gregor has argued that teleological arguments are not primary or even necessary for Kant. They are, she maintains, in *Laws of Freedom*, ch. 9, only meant to make things clearer to the ordinary moral agents of Kant's own day, and so have a purely illustrative force, and could be totally abandoned without essential loss. Kant's main argument, throughout all his derivations of duties from the categorical imperative, is, she holds, the rational argument which seeks to show the system of the essential ends of a rational being with an animal nature, the ends which such a being must rationally will. It just happens that these ends coincide with the purposes of nature far enough to allow Kant to appeal to nature as a short-cut to what he really wants to say. But it is not possible to separate the 'rational' and 'teleological' arguments so sharply. For what a rational being necessarily wills is the preservation and perfection of its essential nature. As soon as one begins to talk of perfecting an essential nature, one is involved in a purposive understanding of human nature, as so constituted that it has a proper fulfilment. One could not abandon this without radically changing the character of Kantian ethics.

Moreover, Kant's reliance on a 'natural law' view of morality is in practice greater than even this might suggest. For, as will be shown more fully in 7.4, he takes the fulfilment of human nature to be expressed in the principle that 'in all the actions which affect himself a man should so conduct himself that every exercise of his powers is compatible with the fullest employment of them'. (LE, 123; Vor. 154.) One should aim at the fullest realisation of purposes; and one cannot will anything which would impair one's ability for the free setting of purposes. But it is a matter for empirical investigation what actions impair one's physical or mental abilities. Suicide obviously does; and if masturbation, drunkenness and gluttony do, then they cannot be willed. Yet one could will all persons to indulge in sensual pleasures, as long as such pleasures did not come to control one's life to such an extent that one's creative pursuit of other purposes was impaired. Indeed, such indulgence might well seem to constitute a fuller employment of one's natural capacities than a policy of asceticism. And to prohibit it seems to be in tension with Kant's view that imperfect duties, at least, allow a certain amount of latitude to act from inclination occasionally. There seems to be no particular reason why the prohibition on sensual indulgence should not be an imperfect one—a prohibition in general, but not in every particular case. What lies behind Kant's attitude in these matters is simply the belief that the purposes of nature should never be frustrated, or misused for the sake of pleasure. This is a much stronger commitment to a 'natural law' view of morality than the principle that a rational being cannot contradict the essential ends of its own nature.

One might well hold that Kant's appeal to the merely biological 'purposes' of nature can be discarded without any basic change to his general ethical theory, even though this would alter the specific derivation of duties which Kant is able to make from the supreme principle of universalisability. But one could not discard the notion of a generally purposive constitution of human nature in the same way; for it is essential to Kant's use of the principle of universalisability that it assumes the existence of essential ends of human nature—the ends, in general, of perfection and happiness—by reference to which the criteria of consistency and contradiction can be formulated. The extraordinary fact that a great many able Anglo-Saxon critics of Kant have failed to see this has no doubt led them to be more scathing about the emptiness and inadequacy of the principle of universalisability than they might otherwise have been. Yet it is probably true that even when it is placed in its fuller context of a purposive understanding of nature, the principle of universalisability which is classically formulated in the first formula of the categorical imperative still fails to provide the detailed derivation of specific duties which Kant claims to have provided in the *Metaphysic of Morals*. Whether or not this is so, it is worth making explicit the point which Kant took for granted in formulating the supreme principle of morality, that practical reason necessarily aims at the preservation and development of all purposes (including the essential purposes with which nature is concerned in man, human happiness and perfection). The supreme principle of morality states the principle in accordance with which reason pursues this aim, and that is what is now often called the principle of universalisability.

7.3 THE PRINCIPLE OF UNIVERSALISABILITY

Kant claims that the first formulation of the categorical imperative—'Act only on that maxim whereby thou canst at the same time will that it should become a universal law'—is the means of deciding what one's duty is, and that all imperatives of duty can be derived from it. (G, 24; Ber. 4, 404. G, 46; Ber. 4, 421.) Commentators have rarely believed this claim; and a short examination of one use of the principle of universalisability will both clarify what Kant meant by it and expose some of its weaknesses.

Consider the example which Kant gives of a man proposing to act on the maxim: 'When I think myself in want of money, I will borrow money and promise to repay it, although I know that I never can do so.' (G, 47; Ber. 4, 422.) When universalised, this maxim would read, 'If in difficulties, make deceitful promises'; or, as Kant puts it, more weakly, 'If in difficulties, it is permissible to promise deceitfully.' Would it be impossible, or self-contradictory, for everyone to adopt such a maxim? Kant holds that it would; but the case is not at all straightforward. Certainly, if everyone always acted on the maxim, 'Always break promises', the institution of promising would cease to exist; for no one could even be taught what a promise was if every promise was always broken. Perhaps a world without the institution of promising would be a better world; but the present purpose of the act of promise-breaking would be self-defeating, since it presupposes that promises will in general be believed. A similar argument works for stealing and lying; for if everyone always stole or lied, the institutions of private property and language could not exist; and so there would not exist such activities as stealing and lying, which presuppose the existence of those institutions.

But one's maxim of action is unlikely to be something like, 'Always break promises'. It is more likely to be, 'Keep promises in general; but break them in difficulties, when you think you can get away with it'—and this is more like the maxim Kant actually suggests. Such a qualified maxim is consistently universalisable. For promising as an institution would still exist—the situation in which a man would be able to break his promise with impunity is after all not so frequent as to undermine the whole institution of promising. There would be less trust in such a society; men would need to check carefully people's liability to break their promises. Similarly, with the universal adoption of qualified maxims of stealing and lying, everyone would be expected to steal or lie whenever they thought they could gain benefit by doing so. Society would be more insecure and its members more suspicious; but there is no reason to think that social life would be made impossible.

But could one will such a society to exist? The answer is probably that some people would, and some would not. Those who are cautious and value security highly might be unable to will such a society to exist. Whereas those who were relatively strong or who valued competition, conflict or the possibility of great gain, even with the risk of failure, would gladly opt for such a society. The universal adoption of such maxims would probably bring about an inequitable society in which the strong would be able to exploit the weak. And this is not just a possible, but an actual state of affairs in most societies; one, moreover, which many people would positively prefer.

But though, as one of the strong, I might be able to will that all men acted on these maxims, could all men agree on this? Could I will it, if I was one of the unfortunate weak? It may seem not; and John Rawls[3] has offered a reconstructive account of Kant's principle which requires that men act as if, before entering a society, and without knowing in advance what their position in society would be, they had mutually agreed on the social rules which would be accepted in that society. The implication is that, since no one would desire to be poor or weak, all would devise a system in which eliminable extremes of poverty or inequality were eliminated. This is the force of one main implication of the third formulation of the categorical imperative: 'So act as to treat humanity, whether in thine own person or in that of any other, in every case as an end withal, never as means only.' (G, 56; Ber. 4, 429.) This formula could be interpreted to mean that one should refrain from interfering with the purposes of others,

---

[3] Cf. J. Rawls, 'Justice as Fairness', in *Philosophical Review* (1958).

and that one should not subject another person to some purpose which he himself could not have willed, or agreed to. This does not mean what he did agree to, or would have agreed to if asked. It means what he would have agreed to, had he been a wholly rational being without partiality for his own situation. In this sense, the formula is derivable from the formula of universal law, as Kant claims. For if a maxim is such that any purely rational being would act on it in a similar situation, whatever their own situation, then all persons may be taken to have given their tacit consent to the maxim. One could then be said to be treating all persons as antecedent co-legislators with oneself, and thus as ends, not means. As the formula of universality gives the form of moral maxims, so the formula of ends-in-themselves provides the matter. (G, 65 f.; Ber. 4, 436.) Laws must be universal for a specific range of subjects; and the formula of ends gives these subjects as persons. Further, the formula of autonomy ('So to act that the will could at the same time regard itself as giving in its maxims universal laws') specifies that these persons must all be capable of being legislators of the law. (G, 63; Ber. 4, 434.) So there is one sense in which all these formulae are 'at bottom only so many formulae of the very same law, and each of itself involves the other two'. (G, 65; Ber. 4, 436.)

The model of antecedent co-legislation, however, does not provide one set of moral rules upon which all men could agree. The procedure requires one to step outside one's own physical and mental being and consider oneself as a purely rational being. So one cannot refer to the sorts of things one actually desires, being the sort of person one is. Considering oneself only as a being with unspecified desires and an unspecified degree of rationality, one must devise rules to regulate one's relations with similar beings. Any rules which could not be assented to by every such being would be prohibited. Even if the supposal of a being choosing without any reference to its actual dispositions and capacities is coherent, it is not clear that all such beings would agree on the rules of the society they would choose.

It may at first seem obvious that all would choose a harmonious, integrated society, in which there was little risk of inequality or failure, and in which all were concerned with the welfare of others; and Kant obviously thought this was the case. But one might consider that lack of integration, conflict and inequality is an essential condition for the genesis of creative genius, originality and inventiveness; and that competition and aggression is responsible for social progress and all that is worthwhile in culture. In his essay on *The Idea For a Universal History*, Kant himself writes, 'Thanks be to Nature, then, for the incompatibility, for heartless, competitive vanity, for the insatiable desire to possess and to rule! Without them, all the excellent natural capacities of humanity would for ever sleep, undeveloped.' (OH, 16; Ber. 8, 21.) Here, he seems to see positive good in the existence of an inequitable and competitive society, in which men's maxims would be those of limited acquisitiveness, lying and promise-breaking.

Given such a view, a man might, on quite disinterested grounds, opt for a system in which there was great inequality and conflict, and yet a great increase in culture and even in the general standard of living. On a less disinterested level, a man might well gamble on coming out on top in a system where the rewards were very great, the risks of failure not too terrifying, and the opportunities to achieve the rewards were more or less equal. Although one would not like to be cheated or lied to, one may still be prepared to opt for a system in which someone had to be lied to and cheated to make great personal rewards possible for some; and to gamble on one's chance of being successful in that system. Even this, many might say, is better than a society in which everyone is 'tied down' to the same level of mediocrity in consumption of goods. After all, if one rules out self-interest for others, one rules it out for oneself too; and in that case one may prefer not to rule it out at all. It seems that Kant did not seriously consider this possibility. But, after all, even the maxim, 'Break general rules when it is in your long-term interests to do so' is quite universalisable, given that it will be in few people's interests to do so very often.

So it seems that some antecedent co-legislators might choose a totally egalitarian society, being very cautious people; while others might choose even an hereditary aristocracy, though they cannot know their own place in the system. They might do so, partly as a gamble, but also partly out of considerations to do with the morale, continuity and culture of society. Such choices are not matters of being more or less reasonable. They are due to differences of temperament; and this focuses attention on a basic weakness of the account in terms of antecedent co-legislators. For the antecedent chooser is supposed to be of unspecified temperament. Kant clearly supposes that differences of the sort mentioned could not arise among wholly rational beings; or that, if they did, they would not be morally relevant. But, as John Kemp says, 'There may be a number of different, but equally rational, ways of systematically allowing for the welfare and needs of human beings, and so, different, but equally rational, ways of life or systems of morality.'[4]

In addition to this difficulty, that equally rational beings might antecedently choose very different societies, there is the further difficulty that what one might antecedently will, if everyone willed the same, might differ from what one would will, knowing that others would will (whether rationally or partially) differently. Kant seems to take account of this, in the *Doctrine of Law*, when he allows that before a civil society is set up, in a 'state of nature', 'no one is under obligation to abstain from interfering with the possession of others, unless they give him a reciprocal guarantee for the observance of a similar abstention from interference with his possession'. (MEJ, 157; Ber. 6, 307.) If one takes this statement to mean what it says, the universalisable maxim of action involved must be something like: 'Whenever there is no legal authority and men attack, it is permissible to defend oneself, or even attack pre-emptively.' If Kant will allow maxims as qualified and specific as this, it seems that moral action will depend very much on what the actual behaviour of other men is. Yet though Kant permits pre-emptive attacks in certain circumstances, the prohibition of all pre-emptive attacks is not only non-self-contradictory, but would be held by some to be morally obligatory, even though it meant death. Here is a moral dispute which appeal to the universality principle cannot settle.

Again, once a civil society has come into being, Kant says, 'It is the duty of the people to bear any abuse of the supreme power, even though it should be considered to be unbearable'. (MEJ, 177; Ber. 6, 320.) Once more, this is a duty which would be vehemently contested by many; so that again it does not seem sufficient to claim to derive it, however indirectly, from the formula of universal law. The situation is that the more particular

---

[4] J. Kemp, *Reason, Action and Morality* (Routledge and Kegan Paul, London, 1964), p. 146.

and context-dependent the maxims of one's action become, the less useful the principle of universalisability becomes, as a test of moral rightness. A particular maxim, like 'Lie whenever you are in an embarrassing situation and it will harm no one to do so', because it is particular, could be universalised quite consistently. Since there is no *a priori* method of setting limits to the specificity of maxims, it will always be possible to find a maxim particular and idiosyncratic enough to be consistently universalised, in any situation. The formula of universal law is, as most critics have agreed, quite unable to provide a sufficient criterion for morally right actions. But it would be wrong to suppose that, when one has said this, one has undermined Kant's ethical theory. Indeed, it would be more correct to say that Kant's own analysis of the supreme principle of morality fails to state adequately his actual account of ethics to such an extent that it is radically misleading. In entailing the claim that all duties can be derived from a purely formal principle, it completely fails to express the close connexion between the concepts of virtue, perfection and happiness which Kant wanted. To understand his ethical theory, one must consequently penetrate behind the terminology in which it is expressed, and which Kant so laboriously invented, to the underlying teleological view, which is frequently and unmistakably outlined in his many published works.

7.4 THE PRINCIPLE OF HUMANITY

In the first *Groundwork* derivation of the duty of beneficence, Kant again appeals to the model of antecedent co-legislation; and he repeats this argument in the *Metaphysic of Morals*. The maxim, 'I will not help others in distress' could be universal, he says; but it could not be willed without contradiction. For, since I could not will to be in need of aid, but deprived of all hope of it, I could not antecedently will a society to exist with such distressed persons in it (for I might turn out to be one of them!). It is true that I could not desire help, and at the same time will to be ignored. But might I not, like the gambler, antecedently will a society in which such people existed—perhaps partly on the grounds that self-sufficiency is a virtue, and beneficence might sap initiative? A distinction must be made here, which Kant does not explicitly make, between 'helping those in distress' and beneficence, in the sense of helping others to achieve their own purposes. Perhaps even the gambler would not will people to be in positive distress, without the possibility of aid. But he might very well will to leave them alone and not positively forward their aims, if they were comfortably placed.

The positive aspect of beneficence is mentioned by Kant in the derivation from the formula of humanity (G, 58; Ber. 4, 430), where he remarks that to take another person as an end in himself is to take his ends as one's own. The furtherance of another's aims cannot be derived from the principle of universal law; and this is one place where it becomes apparent that the third formula in fact adds significantly to the first formula of the categorical imperative, and is not just a restatement or popularised form of it, as Kant claims. To make another's ends one's own is to seek to further his happiness, as he conceives it, and so to aim at one of the essential ends of humanity. To take humanity as an end in itself involves the pursuit of 'the natural end which all men have' (G, 58; Ber. 4, 430), which is happiness; for only in this way can 'humanity' become a goal of action, as opposed to a mere limiting condition on actions which are aimed at other purposes.

In the *Metaphysic of Morals*, Kant derives the further duties of gratitude and sympathy from the general principle of perfecting humanity in others—gratitude because the lack of it tends to undermine the practice of beneficence, and sympathy because it is 'one of the impulses which nature has implanted in us so that we may do what the thought of duty alone would not accomplish' (MM, 126; Ber. 6, 457); and so its cultivation is a means to promoting active benevolence. It would be an exceedingly weak argument that no rational being could will to be part of a system of nature in which no being had 'the will to share in other's feelings', even though there was no one in distress in that system. At least, it would be so unless one assumed that a rational being is essentially and necessarily such as to will the perfecting of rational natures by the free choice of purposes and their fullest realisation in a harmonious society. This is exactly what Kant needs to assume to make his derivation of duties from the supreme principle at all plausible. And this is in fact what Kant explicitly cites in the *Groundwork* as the supreme principle of morality, the principle of autonomy, the principle of being a universal legislator in a kingdom of ends (all ends combined in a systematic whole). (G, 61 f.; Ber. 4, 433.) What is of absolute worth in human life is the obedience to such self-legislation, in independence of all natural desires; commitment to doing only what autonomous reason permits or enjoins, simply because reason permits or enjoins it.

It is axiomatic for Kant that a rational being necessarily wills the fullest realisation of all possible purposes, which are morally permissible. 'The power to set an end—any end whatsoever—is the characteristic of humanity (as distinguished from animality).' (MM, 51; Ber. 6, 392.) Thus such a being cannot fail to will the preservation and development of the power to realise all possible purposes; and this includes the physical and intellectual powers which are a condition of the realisation of fully rational action. To take 'humanity' as an end, in a positive sense, is to cultivate one's natural perfection, as a precondition of all autonomous willing, and of fully rational action.

Kant advocates the pursuit of one's own perfection, not in the sense that the increase of knowledge, say, is to be desired for its own sake, as if it were an intrinsic good (this again would be heteronomy); but in that knowledge is a precondition of free rational action. Every development of intellect, understanding, memory, imagination and physical fitness enlarges one's capacities for the positive and creative use of freedom in setting all sorts of morally permissible purposes for oneself, and helping others to realise their purposes. This is autonomy, the freedom of the will to be self-determining and universally legislative.

Although there are ends which are also duties, it would be a relapse into heteronomy to take these as ends-in-themselves, as intrinsically worthwhile ends. They are, rather, necessary means to developing the ability for the creative pursuit of purposes. It is just this creative ability itself, and the way in which it is exercised, that is unconditionally good, that is the only end-in-itself.

Unfortunately, Kant speaks very confusingly when expounding the notion of an end-in-itself. First, he says that it is 'humanity' which is to be taken as an end-in-itself; and this is the power of freely setting ends, in general. It is to be identified with practical reason, by definition a 'power of ends as such', which always acts on the supreme formal principle of universal legislation: 'Respect always applies to persons only.' (CPR, 79; Ber. 5, 76.) Second, he writes that 'morality, and humanity as capable of it, is that which alone has dignity'. (G, 64; Ber. 4, 435.) And again, 'respect for a person is properly only respect for the law . . . of which he gives us an example'. (G, 21; Ber. 4, 401.) Third, and most famously, he writes, 'Nothing can possibly be conceived in the world, or even out of it, which can be called good without qualification, except the Good Will'; that is, the disposition always to do what practical reason enjoins or permits, because it enjoins or permits it. (G, 10; Ber. 4, 393.) This is what Kant calls the duty of moral perfection, in the *Metaphysic of Morals*: 'the cultivation of one's *will* [moral attitude] to fulfil every duty as such'. (MM, 45; Ber. 6, 387.) Though these vacillations are very confusing, it appears that the intrinsically worthwhile good which Kant was proposing as the foundation of morality was a complex good involving the spontaneous activity of practical reason, its conformity to the principle of universality, and the obedience of the sensuously affected power of choice to its dictates. In the pursuit of this good, one must necessarily be concerned with the ability for setting purposes in general (the duties of natural perfection); the realisation, and consequently, the enjoyment of these purposes (the duty of seeking happiness); and the capacity freely to obey what practical reason wills (the duty of moral perfection). All these ends may be called 'formal', in that they do not mention any specific purposes (except those natural perfections which are a means to increasing one's ability to set purposes in general). It is in this sense that Kant's ethics does not depend on the intuition of moral values or intrinsic goods, though it is fundamentally concerned with purposes and the consequences of human actions. The supreme principle of morality, the principle of autonomy, sets no specific material objectives of action. But it does take, as the only intrinsically worthwhile value, the free setting, pursuit and enjoyment of all possible purposes. As Kant writes, in Reflexion 7251, 'The regulative principle of freedom: that [actions] do not conflict; the constitutive principle: that they reciprocally promote each other for the purpose of happiness.' (Ber. 19, 294.) It is one of the greatest ironies of philosophical criticism that an ethical theory which finds the supreme value of life in creative and spontaneous activity should have been so often characterised as a legalistic recommendation of a grim, dogged obedience to duty for duty's sake, whatever the consequences.

There is one other important strand in Kant's notion of treating humanity as an end-in-itself, and he brings this out in listing perfect duties to oneself and duties of respect to others. We must not simply take others' aims as our own, and aim at the fullest realisation of all possible purposes. We are also obligated to acknowledge 'the dignity of humanity in every other man' (MM, 132; Ber. 6, 462); and here Kant holds that self-importance, slander, ridicule and bodily mutilation are prohibited, as contrary to the dignity of others. One might think that Kant's appeal is to the co-legislation argument again, since others could not will such things for themselves. But that there is more to it than that is made clear by Kant's discussion of duties of respect to humanity in oneself. One must creatively pursue all permissible purposes as fully as possible; but one must do this because one would, if fully rational, naturally will to do so; not because one has a natural inclination to do so. Moral perfection is to do all one's duties (to be perfect) from the motive of duty (to be holy)—though this motive may rarely come to consciousness and be made explicit (cf. MM, 113 f.; Ber. 6, 446 f.). This absolute freedom from the pressures of inclination is involved in autonomy, as giving man his inherent dignity. And it gives rise to the perfect duties to self.

Thus suicide is condemned because it subordinates oneself as a moral agent to desires: 'To dispose of oneself as a mere means to an arbitrary end is to abase humanity in one's own person . . . which was yet entrusted to man . . . for its preservation.' (MM, 85; Ber. 6, 423.) If one treats humanity as an end-in-itself, one cannot subject it to inclinations. Masturbation is similarly prohibited, as a degradation of humanity. And Kant holds that lying 'violates the dignity of humanity in his own person'; for by lying, man 'renounces his personality' and 'annihilates his dignity as a man'. (MM, 92 f.; Ber. 6, 429.) This again is because lying subordinates reason to inclination; and, in self-deceit, by which men conceal from themselves the fact that their maxims are based on inclination, rather than on direct obedience to the moral law, all moral evil finds its origin. Kant also claims to derive from the principle of independence from inclinations, the prohibitions on 'miserly avarice', by which one subjects oneself to riches at the expense of one's true needs, and on servility, by which one fails to exhibit reverence for one's inner worth. Thus, he says, 'be no man's lackey . . . do not accept favours you could do without . . . even a mere cry in bodily pain is unworthy of you . . . kneeling down . . . is contrary to the dignity of humanity'. (MM, 101 f.; Ber. 6, 436.)

Here, Kant moves from respect for one's supreme worth, as a moral being—which one would think hardly any empirical circumstances, however restrictive, could annul—to the advocacy of 'dignity', in the sense of proper pride, or honourableness. But there is no way whatsoever in which one can infer from the principle of willing freely to do only what reason permits or enjoins to the duty of not kneeling in church, crying out in pain, or accepting favours from others. If supreme moral worth consists in the free pursuit of all universalisable purposes, why should such activities as these be thought to undermine human dignity? It seems clear that the principle of humanity is, in practice, not just the principle that one should act from the motive of obedience to reason. It includes the further principle that the intellectual powers have an inherent worth which man's animal nature lacks; so that one must cultivate the intellectual powers and keep the sensual faculties very closely in check. It is because Kant believes that certain sorts of purpose—broadly speaking, sensually orientated purposes—are degrading to rational humanity, that he advocates the cultivation of apathy and self-mastery—the independence from all sensual desires—and the pursuit of a sense of honour, arising from one's consciousness of one's superiority to one's animal nature.

The principle of humanity is thus the most complex of all Kant's formulae of the categorical imperative, and it includes the three main strands of which Kant makes use in his derivation of particular duties from the supreme principle of morality. First, the principle of universalisability is contained in the notion of all rational beings as antecedent co-legislators, so that none can be used solely as a means to furthering the purposes of the others. Second, the positive injunction to take the ends of others as one's own, to pursue as fully and creatively as possible all the purposes one can for oneself, and to develop the purposes of nature in oneself is contained in the notion of 'humanity' as a positive, if formal, goal of action. And third, the distinction between intellectual and sensual powers, and the injunction to achieve independence and mastery of all sensual powers, is to be found implicit in the working out of the notion of the 'dignity of humanity' in oneself and others. It is perhaps partly because the formula of humanity has been neglected by most Kant critics, in favour of the formula of universal law, that the true nature and complexity of Kant's method of deriving particular duties from the supreme principle has rarely been adequately treated.

7.5 THE NATURE OF THE SUPREME PRINCIPLE OF MORALITY

The initial implausibility of Kant's ethics is the thought that one can will something in the absence of any desire whatsoever. But this implausibility can be lessened or overcome if one considers that desires need not be the only fundamental reasons for action. On Kant's view, desires are contingent and particular, whereas morally willable maxims must be necessary and universal ('If a law is to have moral force . . . it must carry with it absolute necessity' (G, 4; Ber. 4, 389)); so one cannot found one's ultimate choices even on a disinterested, universalised desire (what one could *want* all men to do). Moral reasons must be necessary, in the sense that they are necessarily what they are, they could not have been otherwise; not in the sense that they are necessarily pursued. Kant characterises such reasons as those which a fully rational being would necessarily choose. Such goals are not chosen because they are desired, or because they are intrinsically valuable. In this respect, Kant's doctrine is analogous to Calvin's view of morality. For Calvin, what is morally right is what God wills. For Kant, what is morally right is what practical reason (necessarily) wills. This can be stated, in an entirely abstract form, as: what can be prescribed as a universal law for all rational beings is morally right (Formula 1 of the categorical imperative, or the Principle of Co-legislation).

On a less abstract level, considering the general nature of man as a sensuous rational being, with certain basic desires and inclinations, inhabiting a system of natural purposes (nature, teleologically conceived), reason will necessarily prescribe, as a universal law, the preservation and fulfilment of his nature; and, in general, the fullest realisation of all possible purposes of which he is capable (formulae 4 and 5, or the Principle of the Kingdom of Ends). This will include the development of his purposes; the purposes of others, so far as they are compatible with a like freedom of others; and the purposes of nature in him, which lead to the development of 'culture', as a distinctively human characteristic. Finally, the activity of legislative reason must itself be regarded as an intrinsically valuable goal. For sensuous beings, who are continually beset by inclinations, it is always a struggle to ensure that one subordinates oneself freely to the activity of practical reason, whatever one's desires may be. So man, as a sensuous being, is bound to respect humanity in himself, and take obedience to this as his absolute value (formula 3, or the Principle of Humanity). The ultimate moral goal of human life is freely to obey the dictates of practical reason, which is one's true self.

In this scheme, the principle of co-legislation states the abstract principle which governs the choices of all autonomous rational beings. The principle of the kingdom of ends states the application of this principle to a natural world-system in which various purposes are actual or possible. And the principle of humanity states the one intrinsic value for a rational being with sensuous impulses. Underlying all these formulae is what can fairly be called the principle of autonomy—the principle that reason, as a 'power of ends as such', is able to set its own necessary purposes without having to be guided by the contingent occurrence of desires or any dependence on intuition of objective moral values. This, of course, is not a moral principle at all (part of a set of moral rules). It is the basic principle which is the condition of the possibility of having any moral rules at all. To say that reason can set purposes autonomously is to state a fact. The formulae of the categorical imperative set out the formulae according to which reason does this; and therefore they do provide criteria for discovering moral rules.

These formulae are not, however, 'only so many formulae of the very same law', as Kant says. (G, 65; Ber. 4, 436.) As I have tried to show, formulae 4 and 5 add significantly to formula 1, in speaking of the fullest realisation of purposes. Formula 3 adds to this again the assertion of the absolute worth of the good will (obedience to reason). And Kant further restricts the range of permissible purposes by appeal to the notion of the dignity of humanity (from formula 3), which forbids the adoption of sensual purposes, while enjoining those purposes which involve intellectual culture. All these formulations are used in the derivation of duties from the supreme principle of morality.

However far Kant is from his goal of formulating just one supreme principle of morality, and however unsuccessful the derivation of particular duties is, it should be clear that Kant was essentially concerned with human fulfilment, and that he regarded reason as being concerned, not just with non-contradiction and consistency, but with the preservation and development of all possible purposes in a harmonious system. He assumed a teleological notion of nature as a realm of ends. And he maintained the absolute worth of practical reason, its legislation and the will which freely conforms to it. What I have tried to do in this brief account is to show how Kant applied the supreme principle in practice, and to disentangle some of the different strands which are involved in the *Groundwork* formulations of it. Whether Kant's method for stating what constitutes perfection—by asking what a fully rational being could not fail to will—is really less empty than the Wolffian method he complains about (of appealing to nature itself) may be doubted. Though Kant may be right in stressing the place of rational criteria in the development of moral rules, he does not, I have suggested, manage to derive the content of the rules from such formal criteria.

This has seemed so obvious to most critics that some sympathetic interpreters have sought to exempt Kant from criticism on this charge by claiming that he never really meant to derive particular duties from the supreme principle; or at least that he misled both himself and others by trying to do so. As Duncan puts it, 'Nothing more absurd can be imagined' than using the categorical imperative as 'a guide to concrete action'.[5] It was merely a 'curious aberration' on Kant's part which led him to include derivations of particular duties in the *Groundwork*. For all that the supreme principle of morality really states is that, to be a moral judgment, any judgment must be made impartially and universally, in an objective spirit. In citing the formal principle of 'objective commandingness' or 'impartiality', it provides a definition of what morality is; it does not provide a basic principle which is already part of morality. T. C. Williams, also, holds that the categorical imperative, in its main formulation, is really only the principle of impartiality, which clears the way for spontaneous

[5] A. R. C. Duncan, *Practical Reason and Morality* (Nelson, London, 1957), p. 118.

intuitions of particular duties by practical reason.[6] And Schilpp places a similar emphasis on the spontaneous creativity of reason in formulating new moral principles and goals; so that again, the supreme principle only gives a definition of what a moral utterance is; it cannot tell one what one's duty is.[7]

Duncan, Schilpp and Williams have correctly fastened on an idea which is very important in Kant's ethical thinking; namely, the stress on the spontaneous pursuit and realisation of all possible purposes. In doing so, they have placed emphasis on a very much neglected aspect of Kant's thought, and have provided a salutary corrective to the British tradition of Kant criticism which tried to use the categorical imperative as a purely logical criterion from which specific duties could be deduced (so that only those acts were obligatory the contradictories of which were logically self-contradictory). Against this traditional view, it is correct to say that Kant had a much wider, teleological notion of consistency in mind, for which what is important is not logical consistency and inconsistency, but the contribution to or frustration of a universal harmony of purposes, the constitutive purposes of which are to be freely and creatively set and pursued.

Nevertheless, if these views are correct, the whole of the *Metaphysic of Morals* is almost unimaginably absurd, since it sets out to derive the system of human duties in general from the one supreme principle. Moreover, Kant does clearly hold that the class of perfect duties leaves no room for manoeuvre whatsoever; it is fixed, unchanging and universal. There can be no doubt that he takes the imperfect duties of culture and beneficence to be similarly derivable from the supreme principle. It is the specific acts which contribute to fulfilling these maxims which give room for creative spontaneity. One can choose which gifts to develop, whom to help and how. But the maxims themselves are as absolute and unchanging as are perfect duties. So there are definite limits set to creative spontaneity; and the class of human duties is absolute and unchanging. Where do they derive from, if not from the categorical imperative?

The suggestion that they can be creatively prescribed fails to

[6] T. C. Williams, *The Concept of the Categorical Imperative* (Clarendon Press, Oxford, 1968), chaps. 6 and 9.

[7] P. A. Schilpp, *Kant's Pre-Critical Ethics* (Northwestern University Press, Evanston, 1938), chaps. 3 and 11.

allow for the necessity and universality which, for Kant, is characteristic of all moral rules. And the suggestion that they are intuited or somehow derived from nature ignores Kant's explicit rejection of heteronomy, in accordance with which he refuses to found moral laws on any object which could determine the will objectively, even an 'objective', intuited, moral law or value. It also ignores Kant's constant rejection of 'mysticism' in ethics, under which he includes any sort of moral intuition. This leaves reason alone as the source of all particular moral laws. Indeed, given Kant's doctrine that moral laws are necessary, together with his commitment to the epistemological view of the first *Critique*, that all necessary laws must be promulgated by reason itself, and that reason can promulgate only formal laws, it follows that all particular duties must derive from the categorical imperative. But, as has been seen, the particular context, its consequences and the nature of the agent must all be taken into account in formulating one's maxims.

Duncan is right to say that Kant means the supreme principle of morality to be taken as a definition of morality. As Kant says, 'Morality consists then in the reference of all action to the legislation which alone can render a kingdom of ends possible.' (G, 62, Ber. 4, 434.) But this definition also provides a principle which can be applied to particular circumstances to give rise to specific duties; for it states what sort of action will render a kingdom of ends possible—namely, action on a universalisable maxim.

If one wants to preserve a clear distinction between a definition of what morality is, and the supreme moral principle from which all others can be derived, one could say that, for Kant, morality is what a purely rational being would will; and the supreme principle of such willing is the principle of universalisability. Kant combines these two senses of 'principle' in one formula. But whether one thinks that he failed to make the distinction between them because he did not realise there was one, or because he thought it unimportant for his purposes, it is wrong to say that universalisability is meant by Kant to be a definition of morality, and not an ultimate moral principle. In somewhat the same way, it would be wrong to take, 'the greatest happiness of the greatest number' as Mill's definition of goodness and not as a supreme moral principle—even though he may have meant it to be both.

So if one is forced to choose, one should say that the categorical imperative is a moral principle, not a definition of morality. But is there any reason why it could not be both? If there is (if, for example, this would make 'goodness' definable) it is not one which Kant would have accepted. For he did want to define 'goodness' in terms of what a purely rational will would necessarily choose. And knowing this, he thought, one *ipso facto* knew the principle upon which such a will would choose; and that was the supreme moral principle.

I think, therefore, that one cannot reasonably deny that Kant regarded the categorical imperative as a purely formal principle from which particular classes of duties could be derived, when taken in conjunction with the general nature of men. But if Kant's ethics is formalistic, it is a formalism which means to take full account of all natural and human purposes, and of the essential ends of humanity, perfection and happiness. It is certain that his stress on formalism has helped to obscure, for many critics, his concern with the fulfilment and enjoyment of moral purposes. When, for instance, he speaks of the good will as unconditionally good, good without qualification, even if it fails to produce any effects in the world (G, 11; Ber. 4, 394), it would seem as though he was asserting that even if the good will was manifested in an ignorant, emotionally unbalanced and weak-willed being, and so was doomed to inevitable frustration; and even if that being was miserable and in pain throughout the course of his life; even then the mere presence of a good will would be absolutely good. That is, it would be better that such a state should exist than that it should not. But that this is not Kant's view, despite appearances, is made clear just a little later, when he points out that though the good will is the supreme good, the condition of all other goods, including happiness; yet it is 'not indeed the sole and complete good'. (G, 14; Ber. 4, 396.) The unconditional good is what may be distinguished as moral goodness. Since this can only be exemplified by an autonomous rational being, not entirely subject to inclinations, it does have an intrinsic worth. Without its presence, the existence of a sentient being in a state of complete happiness would not have any moral worth. But, as Kant maintains in his discussion of the *summum bonum*, both the element of moral goodness and the element of the ability to realise and enjoy particular purposes—and therefore the goods of talent, temperament and fortune, mentioned at G, 10 (Ber. 4, 393)—are necessary to the existence of the complete good. So, though in particular cases the good will may fail to produce effects, it is not Kant's view that the supposal of a perpetually failing good will is intrinsically valuable, or even that it is coherent. Kant is concerned with the success of moral willing as well as with its supreme worth.

Yet the paradox of Kant's ethics is that, though moral action is thus essentially concerned with the fulfilment of natural and moral perfection, such fulfilment is impossible in this world. I am not always able to act consistently; my desires remain largely recalcitrant to reason; other people rarely have the will and power to do what is right; and nature does not ensure the satisfactory fulfilment of those moral purposes in which true happiness is to be found.

Nevertheless, Kant maintains that it remains 'an inflexible precept of the will' to do what a purely rational being would do in an ideal world, in which all other beings had the will and power to act rightly. (G, 69; Ber. 4, 438 f.) For such a paradoxical view of morality to be intelligible at all, one must postulate that, somehow, nature can be so determined that moral effort will not finally be in vain. Thus God must be postulated, as a being with intellect and will, who can so determine nature that happiness will finally be in accord with virtue; and the immortality of the soul must be postulated, so that the human fulfilment which is not possible in this life may be looked for hereafter. It is essential for an understanding of Kant to see that this paradox is at the heart of his ethical view: that morality is centrally concerned with human fulfilment, which is yet admitted to be impossible in this life. It is sheer misconception to suppose that Kant is not concerned with human flourishing, so that one may thereby avoid both the paradox and the postulates of practical reason by means of which Kant attempts to resolve it.

CHAPTER EIGHT

NATURE AND PURPOSE

8.1 THE BEAUTIFUL AND THE SUBLIME

The teleological context of Kant's ethics can be clearly seen as an integral and essential part of his theory when reason is seen to be closely concerned with the purposes of nature, and yet to subject nature to categorical demands for which nature is of itself unable to provide the conditions of fulfilment. There is an important sense in which nature is not simply neutral to man's moral striving. It provides the conditions for such striving; it presents an obstacle to it, through the presence of the impulses of sensibility; and, though it is always in itself insufficient to allow the fulfilment of the moral end, the *summum bonum*, it yet sets the purposes which reason must preserve and fulfil. This view of nature may seem strangely at variance with the concept of nature as a mechanistic and deterministic system of causally interacting substances, outlined in the first *Critique*. But in the second *Critique*, Kant makes it clear that there must exist a supersensible ground, conceived by means of the concept of God, which is able to harmonise the system of nature with the dictates of morality. And in the *Critique of Judgment*, he outlines a concept of nature which has a much more positive role to play in relating the fields of theoretical and practical reason. He does this by introducing the notion of 'finality', or purposiveness, as a mediating concept between the mechanistic nature of the first *Critique* and the demands of moral freedom.

It is by the use of this concept, expressed both in the 'subjective teleology' of art and the 'objective teleology' of organic purposiveness, that Kant attempts to relate more positively the notions of reason and nature, point to a supersensible ground of their unity, and thus achieve the final coherent picture of reality as an intelligible whole which it had always been the dream of rationalism to possess. In Kant's later works from the third

Critique onwards, it becomes increasingly clear that the 'Critical solution' of the first two *Critiques* could only be a provisional statement of a larger metaphysical design. Armed with the notion of the primacy of practical reason, Kant, at the end of his life, is still attempting to develop a rationalist vision of the universe as an intelligible coherent whole; but one which is dynamic, centred on moral willing and commitment, rather than static, centred on the contemplation of metaphysical perfection, as that of Wolff had been. To attain such a systematic unity, nature and reason had to be much more integrally related than the first two *Critiques* may have suggested. And, in the third *Critique*, Kant uses the concept of finality as a sort of mediating concept which gives hints that the supersensible ground of nature may be able to supply the sort of purposes which morality requires.

In the *Critique of Aesthetic Judgment*, Kant holds that the 'beautiful' is a concept which 'affords absolutely no . . . knowledge of the object'. (CAJ, 71; Ber. 5, 228.) The sense of beauty is simply a disinterested, universal and necessary delight which arises because beautiful forms are conducive to the mutual interplay and enhancement of the faculties of imagination and understanding. Here there is, Kant says, 'purposiveness without purpose'—that is, the manifold forms of beauty have no objective end, and yet they seem as if purposively designed to please men in their intricate detail. This finality is not a quality of the object itself; it is just that the representation of it is 'immediately coupled with the feeling of pleasure' of a distinctive sort. (CAJ, 30; Ber. 5, 189.) Whereas the gratifying is so for all animals, and the good is so for all rational beings; only the beautiful caters for and unites both animal and rational functions in man. So the pleasure of disinterested contemplation is a uniquely human sentiment which both mellows the rigour of the moral law and refines the brutality of animal desires.

It is true that beauty has no intrinsic connexion with morality. Yet Kant holds that 'to take an *immediate interest* in the beauty of *nature* . . . is always a mark of a good soul'; and such a temper of mind is at least favourable to the cultivation of moral feeling. (CAJ, 157; Ber. 5, 298.) When we come across an instance of a beautiful form produced solely by nature, it seems to suggest a ground which could enable us to assume 'a uniform accordance of its products with our wholly disinterested delight'. (CAJ, 159;

Ber. 5,300.) Reason necessarily takes an interest in this law-directed arrangement which yet has no objective end; and this interest is akin to the moral interest which is founded on the objective moral law. Indeed, Kant suggests that it can only arise in a person already disposed to the morally good.

Further, in the production of beautiful forms, nature creates 'cyphers' in which it speaks 'figuratively' with a 'higher meaning'. The beautiful can become a symbol of the moral qualities which reason demands; and it is able to express in an obscure, non-conceptual way, the objective reality of such qualities. Thus the ideal of the beautiful is to be found in man himself, who alone contains the end of his own existence. This ideal is 'the expression of the moral' in the human figure; 'the visible expression of moral ideas that govern men inwardly'. (CAJ, 79, 80; Ber. 5, 235.) Thus Kant believes that moral qualities have proper bodily manifestations; and though these matters are, he says, inexact and not capable of demonstration, there is present here a doctrine of the close inter-relation of the natural and moral realms which may be missed in the first two *Critiques*. For it is clear that Kant is thinking of the material world as being shaped in some way by moral considerations; and that the physical body serves not only as an appearance, but as a symbol of moral character.

Whereas beauty is a 'subjective finality' of imagination and understanding, a quasi-purposive enhancement of their mutually reinforcing interplay, aroused by the form of objects, the sublime is associated with formless or limitless objects. Such representations give rise to the idea of limitlessness; they incite the mind to abandon sensibility and rise to the notion of totality, which is a concept of reason. But this notion can arise solely from the super-sensible faculty of reason and so it assures us that we, as cognitive agents, transcend every standard of sense.

Nature at once overawes us by its might and yet calls us to remembrance that we are superior to the whole of nature, in our moral destiny. Just as we respect the moral law, so, in the feeling of the sublime, we respect 'the idea of humanity in our own self', which is revealed by the supremacy of our cognitive faculties over sensibility, occasioned by representations which call forth the purely rational notion of infinity, and thus point to a super-sensible ground of the unity of nature and reason.

Here Kant echoes the doctrine of the *Theory of the Heavens*,

K

that man is at once at the mercy of nature and yet transcends it both in knowledge and in moral action. So nature, even at its most terrifying, is 'might that has no dominion over us'; 'it challenges our power . . . to regard as small those things of which we are wont to be solicitous'. (CAJ, 109; Ber. 5, 260. CAJ, 111; Ber. 5, 262.) Sublimity is not properly a characteristic of nature at all; but of our minds, in so far as we become conscious of our moral superiority to nature. Both the beautiful and the sublime, then, point to a higher ground of nature, which may be partially symbolised in nature but finally lies completely beyond it. And the experience of both has affinities with moral experience. 'The beautiful prepares us to love something . . . apart from any interest; the sublime to esteem something highly even in opposition to our [sensible] interest.' (CAJ, 119; Ber. 5, 267.) Morality is more akin to the sublime than the beautiful, to respect than love. For love still belongs to nature, as a natural inclination; but reason must absolutely dominate nature.

In contemplating beautiful forms, the mind becomes conscious of an elevation above mere sensibility, of a supersensible ground which somehow binds together understanding, sensibility and practical reason; and so the beautiful 'indirectly presents' the morally good. Taste will be perfected, therefore, only when 'sensibility is brought into harmony with moral feeling'. (CAJ, 227; Ber. 5, 356.)

Thus Kant concludes the *Critique of Aesthetic Judgment* with the reflection that 'taste is, in the ultimate analysis, a critical faculty that judges of the rendering of moral ideas in terms of sense'. (CAJ, 227; Ber. 5, 356.) Particular intuitions are taken as symbols of rational, moral, ideas. In the concepts of the beautiful and the sublime, then, nature is able to symbolise the moral reality of the intelligible realm, and lead the mind beyond it to an apprehension of its own inherent transcendence of nature. Thus in aesthetic experience one finds hints of a positive and integral relation between nature and reason which expresses a deeper underlying ground of the supersensible unity of both.

8.2 THE REGULATIVE PRINCIPLE OF TELEOLOGY

There is another way in which nature can be conceived as integrally related to reason through the concept of purposiveness; and

that is in the existence of biological organisms. Kant has un-
covered two sorts of finality in nature—first, that exhibited in the
general possibility of discovering a connected system of laws in
nature; and second, that exhibited in the special characteristic of
some forms of nature to strengthen the mental powers in the
contemplation of beauty. But these are both forms of 'subjective
finality'; they give no ground for positing a causality according to
ends in nature itself. A third sort of finality may be asserted,
which is the objective finality of biological organisms, by which
things in nature do stand to one another as means to ends.

Thus 'a thing exists as a physical end if it is . . . both cause and
effect of itself' (as when a tree reproduces itself), and if 'its parts
. . . are only possible by their relation to the whole'. (CTJ, 18;
Ber. 5, 370 f. CTJ, 20; Ber. 5, 373.) In fact, the parts must be
reciprocally both cause and effect of their form so that 'the nexus
of efficient causes might be no less estimated as an operation
brought about by final causes'. (CTJ, 21; Ber. 5, 373.) Each part
exists for the sake of the others and of the whole, and yet it is
brought about by these others.

In considering the objective teleology of organisms one is
not justified in applying a constitutive principle of teleological
causation; rather one may only apply a regulative principle for the
use of reflective judgment in investigating nature. Thus organisms 'cannot be thought possible except as ends' (CTJ, 24; Ber.
5, 375); but thinking in terms of ends is simply a mode of
reflecting on nature which is purely regulative, and tells nothing
about the constitution of things in themselves. Though the
regulative principle of teleology is 'a mere subjective principle for
the employment of our cognitive faculties' (CTJ, 35; Ber. 5,
385), it must nevertheless supplement the principle of efficient
causality, in the case of organisms.

Kant resolves what he terms the antinomy of teleological
judgment—that nature must be estimated as possible solely on
mechanical principles and also according to final laws—by
reducing both principles to principles of estimation of possibility,
which do not commit one to asserting how things are really
possible. So his position is that both mechanistic and final
principles are subjective and regulative—though indeed the
former principle is a condition of the possibility of any knowledge
of nature (as shown in the first *Critique*); they are the only prin-

ciples by which human reason can understand nature, not necessarily the principles of its real possibility. So it is possible that the 'unknown inner basis of nature' may combine the two seemingly incompatible sorts of causality in a single principle, unknown to us. Kant states here what Bohr was to develop into the principle of complementarity—that two principles, seemingly incompatible, are only so because of the limited nature of human cognition, and may in fact cohere in a single principle, which our cognitive faculties are unable to grasp.

Following the lead set by the understanding of particular parts of nature in terms of teleology, we are led to apply the teleological principle to the whole of nature, regarding it as a system of ends; to subordinate mechanical causality to a general teleological principle; and ultimately to conceive a final end, which would contain its reason for being in itself, and so give meaning and purpose to the whole of nature, and which could not be regarded as a product of nature, or an object of natural science.

Kant writes that, as far as our reason goes, we must postulate final causality as arising from an 'architectonic understanding', distinct from nature. He rejects any theory of purely random change and the Spinozistic view on which the world derives from some unknown ground of necessity. This, he thinks, leaves only theism—the view that the world originates from 'an intelligent Being producing with design'—as the principle of reflective explanation of the possibility of final ends in nature. (CTJ, 43; Ber. 5, 392.) But this is a purely subjective principle of reflection, 'a mere idea to which we in no way undertake to concede reality'. (CTJ, 40; Ber. 5, 389.) The real ground of natural finality remains unknown to us.

However, Kant reiterates that, though teleology leads one to the idea of an intelligent cause, it can by no means lead to the idea of a single omniscient and infinitely good God who has one final end in view. Only ethics can postulate such a being as a condition of the possibility of the *summum bonum*; and physical teleology only serves to give rational ideas an 'incidental confirmation' in physical ends. The possibility of the *summum bonum* as the final end of nature cannot be established theoretically, even for reflective judgment (i.e. as a regulative principle to govern investigation into nature). For 'a final end is simply a conception of our practical reason'—its only possible use is for practical, not theoretical, reason. (CTJ 124; Ber. 5, 454.) But, in this respect, the nature of our reason is such that we must postulate God, though only 'for the practical employment of our reason'. (CTJ, 125; Ber. 5, 456.) We must conceive the attributes of God by analogy, but we do not thereby actually ascribe them (speculatively) to God. Rather, we 'seek to use them for determining our own selves and our will' in a purely practical fashion. (CTJ, 127; Ber. 5, 457.) That is, the concept of 'God' is a model, constructed by analogy, the only proper use of which is to determine our will; we thereby make absolutely no assertion about the conditions of the objective possibility of the things which we are so compelled to conceive, subjectively and practically.

The principle of objective teleology in understanding the natural phenomena of organic life is thus a very restricted one. It has no place in physical science at all; and even for the reflective understanding the concept of 'God' must remain a regulative model, which then requires the addition of moral considerations to furnish the concept of one omniscient, benevolent deity. Nevertheless, such limited considerations lead the mind to think of nature as purposively, and to that extent rationally, ordered; and to go on to form a teleological estimate of nature as a whole. Such an estimate enables Kant to construct a vision of nature as having an historical purpose which plays an essential part in the full expression of the reality of the intelligible world.

8.3 THE HISTORICAL PURPOSE OF NATURE

Accordingly, in the third *Critique*, Kant sets out a view of nature as an evolutionary, self-generating system; but he holds that 'we do not find in it, as nature, any being capable of . . . being the final end of creation'. (CTJ, 88; Ber. 5, 426.) Man appears to be the *ultimate* end of nature, the end to which all other natural things are subordinated. But he can only be a *final* end, an end valuable in itself, by virtue of his moral capacity; and, in the use of this capacity, man entirely transcends nature. His destiny *vis à vis* nature cannot be simply to attain happiness—first, because man's idea of happiness is so fluctuating and indefinite that he cannot construct general laws for attaining it; second, his own nature would never be satisfied with any purely physical goal; third, nature seems in any case indifferent to man's inclinations;

and fourth, man's own nature leads to discord, war, hatred and ruin. Thus he cannot be satisfied by means of nature, either within or without himself.

The end or purposes with which nature is concerned in man must therefore, Kant suggests, be the 'skill for all manner of ends for which he may employ nature', which Kant terms 'culture'. (CTJ, 92; Ber. 5, 430.) Man, though a product of nature, can set before himself deliberately chosen ends, which are 'self-sufficing independently of nature'—i.e. those moral ends which are enumerated in the *Metaphysic of Morals*, together with all the purposes which are permissible in a universal kingdom of ends. Man must posit his own moral ends, not wait to receive them from nature. This he can do only by using the formal moral law to decide ends independently of natural inclinations. In this way man sets his own moral ends. It is the aptitude to bring about these ends of freedom that Kant terms 'culture'.

The ultimate end of nature is not the production of happiness and not the production of a relatively independent being which can control external nature. It is rather the production of a being with moral, free, capacities. This is the end to which nature itself must be conceived as striving; yet nature alone cannot produce the final end, the good and happy will. Only man, in free moral action, can do that.

Kant goes some way towards trying to expound the teleology of nature in this respect. In paragraph 22 of the *Critique of Teleological Judgment*, he foreshadows the Hegelian account of nature as evolving towards its end of culture—providing the conditions in which moral freedom can be realised—through violent evolutionary struggle. (CTJ, 92 ff.; Ber. 5, 429 ff.)

He sketches the growth of a large class of workers, who provide a leisured elite with the opportunity of forwarding culture. With the growth of luxury, class-antagonism and social violence arise; 'yet this splendid misery is connected with the development of natural tendencies in the human race'. (CTJ, 95 f.; Ber. 5, 432.) Nature strives towards the ideal of a civil community which shall be world-wide, where a central authority can regulate the striving of individuals, in which the 'greatest development of natural tendencies can take place'.

In this process, struggle and violence play an essential part, and even war itself is 'a deep-seated, maybe far-seeing, attempt on the

part of supreme wisdom . . . to prepare the way for a rule of law';
a federation of states. (CTJ, 96; Ber. 5, 453.) Thus nature itself,
which provides our animal natures, leads us to transcend them in
the development of 'higher ends than it can itself afford', through
struggle against inclinations. The development of culture, and all
the growth of the arts and sciences, produces civilised men. And
though this does not make men morally better, it does prepare the
way for the total sovereignty of reason which morality will bring,
by disciplining the senses and bringing them under the control of
reason. Even the evils of nature and of man's own temperament
arouse him to opposition and progress and 'at the same time
quicken in us a sense that in the depths of our nature there is an
aptitude for higher ends'. (CTJ, 97; Ber. 5, 434.) So nature leads
mankind, by its own devious methods, towards the development
of a federation of world-states and towards the disciplining of the
inclinations, in the development of intellectual culture. And these
are the preconditions of the existence of a truly moral community, a realised kingdom of ends.

The value of life, if measured by the sum of our enjoyment, is
'less than nothing'. Life receives a certain value from what we do,
in becoming cultured. But still we are thus far only means to 'the
end pursued by nature itself, though it be not our end'. (CTJ, 96;
Ber. 5, 432.) The absolute worth of life must be assigned by us,
by what we do with a view to an end independent of nature, so
that nature itself can only have an end if there is such a final end
transcending it. The final end of the world must exist necessarily
as the final end of an intelligent moral cause, and depend on
nothing but its own free action. Only men, *qua* noumena, can act
on laws by which they determine an end which is absolutely
unconditioned, independent and necessary; the end in question is
the *summum bonum*. Man's existence therefore inherently involves
the highest end; but only in so far as he is a moral being. The
purpose of nature alone, in developing a world-federation and a
civilised, cultured human nature, must always fall short of the
final end which alone gives the whole process meaning, the
realisation of the *summum bonum*.

8.4 ESSAYS ON HISTORY

This conception of the historical purpose of nature is further amplified in a number of essays which Kant wrote at various times between 1784 and 1795. It is worth noting the common viewpoint expressed in these essays, and the fact that the first one to be mentioned was published before the *Groundwork*, so that they do not represent senile aspects of Kant's thought, but opinions which he held even while publishing the Critical philosophy and revising the second edition of the *Critique of Pure Reason*. They help to make clear the extent to which Kant always adopted a teleological view of nature, as the foundation of his ethics.

In 1784, in the *Berlinische Monatsschrift*, Kant published an essay on *An Idea for a Universal History from a Cosmopolitan Point of View*, and many of his remarks on the historical process to be made in the third *Critique* are elaborated here. He holds that there may be a definite natural plan in history, the goal of which is, in detail, as yet unknown, and in which individuals, in following their own purposes, in fact play an essentially subsidiary role. He even hazards a guess that nature might one day produce her own historical interpreter, as she created Newton to explain her causal laws.

The essay sets out nine theses; and the main ones are worth surveying. First, 'All natural capacities of a creature are destined to evolve completely to their natural end.' (OH, 12; Ber. 8, 18.) This is the teleological postulate, that nothing exists in vain. But it clearly does not apply to individual members of a species, many of which are defective or die unfulfilled; and so the second thesis is that in man, the natural capacities directed to the use of his reason are to be fully developed 'only in the race, not in the individual', and through countless generations. Third, 'Nature has willed that man . . . should partake of no other happiness or perfection than that which he himself . . . has created by his own reason.' (OH, 13; Ber. 8, 19.) Man uses reason to bring about 'culture'—which unites 'happiness' and 'perfection'—and thus to transcend the 'merely mechanical ordering of his animal existence'. Nature seems to aim not at mere well-being, but at the rational self-esteem which man has through striving for a perfection and happiness which, it seems, only a later generation can reap. Again, Kant's use of the notion of 'perfection' as a mediating concept between 'duty' and 'happiness' should be noted, as it emphasises the underlying teleological character of his ethical system—a character which may be overlooked if a simple two-fold dichotomy of 'duty' and 'happiness' is assumed.

But man's striving for perfection is not without obstacles; and nature develops individuals' capacities by means of 'their antagonism in society'. Men have an 'unsocial sociability', by which societies evolve through creative strife. Competition both strengthens society and creates divisions within it, Kant holds. Without such selfish, competitive tendencies, 'all talents would remain hidden, unborn in an Arcadian shepherd's life'. (OH, 15; Ber. 8, 21.) 'Man wishes concord; but nature knows better; she wills discord.' (OH, 16; Ber. 8, 21.) The goal of evolution is 'the achievement of a universal civic society'; though Kant doubts whether from 'such crooked wood' as human nature anything straight can ever be built. The 'secret plan' of nature is to bring forth such a state, as 'the only condition in which the capacities of mankind can be fully developed'. (OH, 21; Ber. 8, 27.) But many wars and 'reformative revolutions' are necessary to that end.

The theory that progress is achieved through evil and suffering is developed in the essay *On the Conjectural Beginning of Human History*, published in 1786. Kant traces a conjectural ascent of man from animality to humanity, in four stages. First, man discovered a power of choice, about the 'extent to which to serve impulse', and which impulse to serve. With this, came a certain 'anxiety and alarm' at this power over instinctual drives. Second, he discovered the power of imagination and reason to create artificial desires or prolong and transmute ordinary desires. Here came 'the passage from merely sensual to spiritual', from desire to love, from the agreeable to the beautiful; and, indeed, the first promptings of morality, in a primitive sense of 'decency', which conceals from others what might lower their esteem, and so lays the foundation for sociability and 'manners'. Thirdly, man began to envisage the future; and this, besides making rational planning possible, greatly increased human anxiety about his existence. Fourthly, man took the decisive step of recognising in himself the end of nature. Thereby he was released 'from the womb of nature'; and reason henceforth irresistibly impelled him to develop his natural capacities through toil and struggle, until he made himself worthy of, not passive, but active, self-won, deserved happiness and perfection.

Kant's general thesis is that 'man's departure from that paradise . . . was nothing but the transition from an uncultured, merely animal condition to the state of humanity'. (OH, 59 f.; Ber. 8, 115.) Thus 'the Fall' is an inevitable stage in the development of mankind. But for the individual, it is still a fall, a conflict of reason with animality in which the individual succumbs to evil: 'For the individual . . . this whole change was a loss; for nature, whose purpose with man concerns the species, it was a gain.' (OH, 60; Ber. 8, 115 f.) In man, there is and always will be a conflict between the inclinations of nature (animality) and those, which nature has also given him, which lead to the fulfilment of a moral destiny and govern the growth of culture and civilisation. Conflict is a necessary part of nature's plan; and yet each individual bears the full responsibility for his own moral failures and insufficiencies.

Kant thus attempts to combine a belief in personal responsibility for conflict and suffering with the belief that suffering is an inevitable part of nature's 'secret art'. Man 'abuses reason in its very first act'; yet nature (which one may call providence) ensures that the human race as a whole will evolve to the good, and in this progress gives every man the opportunity to contribute his share. Now, as in his very earliest writings, Kant asserts that man 'must admire and praise the wisdom and purposiveness of the whole', even while involved in wickedness and suffering. (OH, 60; Ber. 8, 116.) In *Perpetual Peace*, written in 1795, he writes that 'Nature inexorably wills that the right should finally triumph', but she brings this about by using one's selfish inclinations to bring about a universal federation of states, which will preserve peace—'Nature guarantees perpetual peace by the mechanism of the human passions.' (OH, 113, 114; Ber. 367, 368.)

Kant accordingly sees history as progressing towards the establishment of a universal federation of states, in which good will triumph within history. In *The Strife of the Faculties*, of 1798, he even takes the alleged universal sympathy towards the French Revolution as a proof of such an eventual triumph of good. However, in a review of Herder, Kant asserts, 'The philosopher would say that the destination of the human race in general is perpetual progress, and its perfection is an . . . idea of the goal to which . . . we have to direct our efforts'. (OH, 51; Ber. 8, 65.) Thus he seems to waver between saying that a perfect commonwealth will sometime be achieved and that it is only an asymptotic Idea, to spur men to endless progress.

Running in parallel with this doctrine of an evolutionary advance of the species is the postulate of the immortality of individual souls, which leave this world at death and thenceforth progress to infinity elsewhere. So, for nature individuals are only transitory parts in its historical advance, fulfilling a necessary role in a universal plan; while for the individual moral agent, nature is only a stepping-stone to an eternal destiny which the individual freely and unpredictably chooses. This vision, with the tension of necessity and freedom which it embodies, is unmistakably the same as that which inspired Kant's earliest works; and so it can be seen how, in a fundamental way, the Critical philosophy left his basic beliefs untouched.

This view of nature as embodying concepts of purpose in anthropology, art, biology, and history underlies and gives sense to the better known ethical doctrines which are sketched in the *Groundwork*. Without it, the distinctive notion of 'duty' which is embodied in the formulae of the categorical imperative would be unintelligible. And yet, though nature has its own purposes, its own 'secret plan'; and although these are important to morality; nevertheless the individual transcends the whole scheme of nature in his 'attachment to this concept of duty for its own sake and without regard to hope of a similar response from others'. (OH, 123; Ber. 8, 376.) Ultimately even the inscrutable wisdom and purpose of nature's evolution is subordinated to the absolute value of the individual and his moral destiny; and without this there is no value in nature whatsoever.

Thus in the end Kant rejects the Wolffian metaphysics, for which the individual plays a necessary, determined part in the overall scheme of the best of all possible worlds. Without renouncing rationalism as such, he places the individual and his personal destiny at the centre of things, and nature and its purposes in a strictly subordinate position. So one is led ultimately to a teleology which is not that of nature but of the moral realm itself.

CHAPTER NINE

MORALITY AND RELIGION

9.1 THE DOCTRINE OF INNATE EVIL

In *Religion Within the Limits of Reason Alone*, written in 1793, Kant develops further his notion of how 'morality leads ineluctably to religion' (Rel. 5; Ber. 6, 6), and of the way in which the metaphysical context of the categorical imperative is to be conceived.

He begins with an unequivocal rejection of the doctrine of the *Lectures on Ethics*, that religious belief can be an incentive to moral action. He now says, 'Morality does not need religion at all ... either to know what duty is or to impel the performance of duty.' (Rel. 3; Ber. 6, 3.) Duty can be known and fulfilled without any reference to considerations of religion. But at once a difficulty becomes apparent with this uncompromising statement. For moral weakness and failure are so widespread and even inevitable that it seems almost naïve to suppose that anyone can wholly fulfil their duty. The situation of apparently inevitable moral failure is one that stands in need of explanation, for a Kantian view of ethics. The importance of the *Religion* is largely that it does attempt to provide such an explanation; and, in doing so, it locates one central way in which morality, though autonomous, yet inevitably leads to religion.

Kant approaches the problem of moral evil by recalling the general Critical doctrine that the free moral acts of human agents express a noumenal, timeless, choice, which is made once for all and is the ground of all temporal moral choices (cf. 5.2). So one must envisage the whole course of a man's life as simply expressing one 'act' of 'intelligible choice', 'the ground antecedent to every use of freedom in experience'. (Rel. 17; Ber. 6, 22.) Although, phenomenally speaking, men can be partly good and partly bad, in reality the ultimate choice of the will can only be for or against the moral law; and thus, judged by pure reason, man must be totally good or bad, in every respect.

From the plain fact that men constantly perform evil acts, one can only infer that they have chosen, as their ultimate maxim, moral evil. Furthermore, 'the ultimate subjective ground of all maxims . . . is entwined with and, as it were, rooted in humanity itself'. (Rel. 27 f.; Ber. 6, 32.) Though every individual is inscrutably free to have chosen otherwise, it is yet the case that all men have chosen evil. There is, Kant holds, a radical innate evil in human nature; though we ourselves must be held responsible for it, antecedently to every use of freedom within experience.

How can one conceive the possibility of such a universal ultimate evil choice? Having established that man must create his own moral character by a free decision for or against the moral law, one can characterise that ultimate moral choice as being either to incorporate the moral law into one's ultimate maxim, which will then cover every particular human act; or to refuse to do so. But how is such a refusal possible?

Kant attempts to answer this question by a consideration of the original constitution of human nature. First, he enumerates three original predispositions towards good in human nature—predispositions which are necessarily involved in human being, and which cannot be finally extirpated. These are: (a) to animality—to preserve oneself and propagate and care for one's offspring; (b) to humanity—the social impulse to acquire worth in the opinion of others; and (c) to personality—the capacity for respect for the moral law as a sufficient incentive. The moral law, says Kant, *is* personality; and the subjective reason for adopting 'respect for law' into our maxims is the predisposition to the furtherance of personality, which he is even prepared to call 'true self-love'. It is when man respects the moral law that he becomes fully a person.

But man also has a propensity to evil in his nature—a 'propensity' being a 'subjective ground of the possibility of an inclination'. (Rel. 23; Ber. 6, 28.) That is, one's maxims can deviate from the moral law, in these ways: first, by frailty, one may be weak in observing the law; second, by impurity, one can mix moral and non-moral motives; third, by wickedness, one may just choose evil maxims. This propensity is universal and innate; its foundation is the free intelligible adoption of a supreme maxim, and so man is responsible for it, and it is not deducible from the concept of man as such.

But whence does the possibility of evil arise? It cannot arise from sensibility, which is morally neutral; nor from a perversion of practical reason, which is impossible. No man can renounce obedience to the moral law entirely, either by considering himself exempted from it, or by the power of his natural inclinations, or by denying its authority altogether. Yet man does depend on sensuous incentives as well as those of reason; and to take these as wholly adequate would be to give rise to moral evil. In every human act, the incentives of one's sensuous nature and the moral incentive must both be adopted into one's maxim. Virtue and wickedness are determined by 'which of the two incentives he [man] makes the condition of the other'. (Rel. 31; Ber. 6, 36.) If self-love is made the condition of obedience to the moral law, then an evil maxim results; so that a man may be evil, even though his empirical character is good. Wicked acts may be lawfully good; what makes them wicked is that they 'reverse the ethical priority among the incentives of a free will'. (Rel. 25; Ber. 6, 30.) Self-deception may well then arise, so that a man may not realise his own true dispositions, but regard himself as perfectly moral. It is for this reason that men need continually to hold before themselves the ideal of inner virtue, in all its purity.

Thus man has a natural propensity to evil which is freely chosen; radical, corrupting all particular maxims; and indestructible, since it is a fundamental intelligible choice. The human heart may not be diabolic; but it is perverse, through frailty and failure to make the moral law the sole motive of action. The 'foul taint of our race' is revealed most fully in 'bourgeois morality', which conforms to outward law, and deceives itself as to the true order of incentives for action.

Kant here seems to commit himself fully to the Christian doctrine of original sin; and his version of the theory retains all the paradoxes of the orthodox account. Evil is innate; but man is responsible for it. It is ineradicable, but every particular action is original and totally free; so each new evil act is an original fall from innocence. He accepts the biblical story of the Fall, treating it as a temporal allegory depicting a non-temporal, intelligible reality. In human existence, the moral law appears as a prohibition, since man is tempted by sensuous incentives. Kant supposes that man may first have questioned the strictness of the law; and then substituted conformity to law for obedience; and finally adopted sensible springs as his determining maxims. In thus deciding to follow the moral law, but as a means to his own long-term ends, he reversed the ethical order of incentives, and moral evil came into being.

This is the existential genesis of the Fall in every man; Adam is a symbol to explain our innate evil propensity. But if one asks again why all men have chosen this course, the ultimate answer must be that there is 'no conceivable ground of moral evil'; such ultimate choices are absolutely inexplicable. Kant does suggest, however, that temptation of the flesh may be an alleviation of guilt; the picture of temptation by Satan conveys that man was seduced and is not fundamentally corrupt. Though man has a corrupted heart, he yet possesses a good will; and so hope remains of a return to the good. Kant holds, then, that the theory of the Fall is true, though not as history. The biblical account may be put to moral use. But the theory is also discoverable by reason without the aid of revelation.

9.2 THE DOCTRINE OF CONVERSION

Kant is thus left with a theory on which, since we ought to be moral, this must be in our power. Yet 'what we are able to do is in itself inadequate', and at best only renders us susceptible of higher, though inscrutable, assistance. (Rel. 40; Ber. 6, 45.) Since man has made his intelligible choice for evil and cannot escape it, he stands in need of Divine assistance; and yet Kant says, 'By reason of the dignity of the idea of duty, I am unable to associate grace with it.' (Rel. 19; Ber. 6, 23.) Any divine assistance there may be must be regarded as an incomprehensible supplement to moral endeavour, which we cannot adopt into our maxims either for theoretical or practical use, and of which there can be no direct experience.

What is needed, in fact, is not a reform in one's particular acts, which is impossible, but a complete reversal of the ordering of incentives we have intelligibly chosen, a conversion of the intelligible act, so that the moral law can be re-established as the sole adequate incentive of all our maxims. What is needed is 'a new creation'; not a gradual reformation, but a noumenal conversion. (Cf. Rel. 43; Ber. 6, 47.) We cannot conceive the possibility of such a conversion, but we must postulate it, because the moral law continues to make absolute demands upon us; and so it must be possible to fulfil them. Given such a conversion, one will not suddenly become ethically perfect; one still starts from a tendency to evil, which must be continually counteracted. But one may begin on an 'endless progress to holiness'. The once-for-all noumenal revolution appears in time as a gradual and infinite reformation; but to God it will be a conversion to goodness in the ultimate ground of all willing.

The infinite being sees in infinite moral progress 'a whole conformable to moral law'. (CPR, 127; Ber. 5, 123.) An ever-defective but endless advance may be judged by an intellectual intuition to be perfect as a whole, because of its underlying disposition, since one's failures must be judged 'inseparable from the existence of a temporal being as such'. (Rel. 61; Ber. 6, 67.) As phenomenon, man is permanently deficient; yet, as noumenon, he is essentially holy, through the change of heart. Unfortunately, one can never be certain such a conversion has occurred; one can only infer it from one's actual moral improvement in life. The hope for forgiveness without moral improvement, on condition merely of a declaration of repentance, is delusory. Salvation must be won through one's own efforts. Even then, it is possible that future improvement may not outweigh past sins; we must observe the whole infinite series of our acts before we can reliably infer to the intelligible disposition underlying them.

The possibility of such a conversion does seem opposed to the fact of our innate corruption. But its possibility is established by the fact that the moral law continues to command categorically; and what one ought to do, one must be able to do. Nevertheless, as all men begin from a state of innate evil, they begin from an infinite debt, which merits eternal punishment (since it lies in the eternal, ultimate disposition). This debt cannot be paid by any other person; nor can it be wiped out by conversion, since no subsequent moral goodness can ever wipe out past evil. How, then, can it be paid?

Kant proposes that the (endless) punishment due to the 'old man', i.e. the innate sinful disposition of all men, is visited upon the 'new man', after the noumenal change of heart, in the form of the world's natural ills. This must not be construed as an innocent man suffering the punishment due to a guilty one. One must conceive the punishment 'as carried out *during* the change of heart itself'. (Rel. 67; Ber. 6, 73.) Thus the whole earthly life of man must be conceived as the temporal expression of a change of heart, one intelligible act—'There are not two moral acts . . . but only a single act.' (Rel. 68; Ber. 6, 74.)

The new man undertakes the punishments due to the old, in the act of changing from one to the other, and thus the new birth is at the same time an act of vicarious sacrifice—the Christian story of Jesus on the Cross symbolises this essentially personal, individual process. Each man is a sort of dual will, one man that he is becoming, and one 'whom he is continually putting off'. What are punishments for one, *qua* sinner, become 'opportunities for the testing and exercising of his disposition to goodness' for one *qua* regenerate. (Rel. 65; Ber. 6, 75.) Only by this means, Kant holds, can one continue to talk of the necessity of having a pure moral disposition in a world wherein it is so plainly impossible—or, in the language of the Christian myth, only so can Divine justice and man's hope for forgiveness be reconciled. So the 'death of the old man' is 'a sacrifice and an entrance upon a long train of life's ills'; and 'only the supposition of a complete change of heart allows us to think of the absolution . . . of the man burdened with guilt' and makes hope possible in the situation of constant moral failure. (Rel. 71; Ber. 6, 76.)

The difficulties of this account are only too apparent. Suppose that at one time, T1, a man has happiness as his determining incentive; at T2 he takes the moral law as incentive; and at T3 he returns to happiness. Has he had a change of heart and back again? For Kant, man must be totally good or bad; so how does one determine the ultimate maxim—by counting empirical acts and balancing them up? Again, how can there be a change of heart in a timeless, unchanging intelligible world? Or how can infinite progress really be equivalent to actual perfection? Can we be sure that all men are regenerate? That the process is one-way and will be completed? If the punishment is infinite, must the new man sacrifice for eternity? And how can one man intelligibly decide both ways at once?

Many of the difficulties spring from Kant's doctrine of transcendental idealism, which does not allow the 'real' world to contain temporal relations. But further difficulties arise from his constant refusal to regard grace as entering constitutively into the moral life.

L

Thus he holds that, even though we begin from a condition of innate evil, yet we must aim at *self*-improvement through moral effort; religious ideas which stress human impotence are, he writes, 'corrupt'. Kant constantly associates prayers for Divine grace with servility, excuse-making and admissions of impotence. He regards worship as favour-currying and specifically condemns fanaticism—the search for inward experience; superstition—belief in miracles; illumination—claims to supernatural insight; and thaumaturgy—using the supernatural as a tool, as in inter-cession. Most of the devotional practices of Christianity are here condemned; and yet Kant claims to have preserved the essence of Christianity in his 'moral religion'. For Kantian religion, everyone must try as much as possible to be good. If God helps, it is in inscrutable ways, and he only helps those who help them-selves. As we cannot see ourselves becoming perfect, we may think of Divine grace helping us in unknown ways. The notion of 'grace' is a completely empty notion which merely attempts to 'explain' our moral incapacity and remove difficulties in the way of accepting the moral law. It cannot be a substitute for even an experienced complement to moral endeavour.

But if this religion is really rather far removed from orthodox Christianity, it would be a mistake to think of it as pure moralism, a form of incitement to constant moral effort. For in the doctrine of innate evil Kant adds a significant and peculiarly religious dimension to his general view of ethics. He still holds that 'the original moral predisposition . . . announces a divine origin' making man aware of the sublimity of his moral destiny. (Rel. 44 f.; Ber. 6, 49 f.) But now he adds that man can be equally aware of an innate corruption and an innate guilt, for which he is himself in some way responsible, and which requires the hope of conversion and a power of grace, albeit inscrutable, to preserve the moral imperative in its purity.

This vision of the moral life as a warfare of good and evil in which ultimate and significant choices must be continually made anew is a deeply religious one. Nature provides only the stage for this battle; the *summum bonum* must be won by desperate struggle and internal conflict; and the conditions which can ensure the possibility of ultimate triumph must be postulated. Religious doctrines are implied in morality in so far as they symbolise this struggle, its origin and its outcome, in the individual life. In so far as they make historical or factual assertions, however, religious doctrines are either superfluous, absurd or even inimical to true morality, since they may lead men to value theoretical beliefs above moral effort.

Perhaps the main factor which does render the *Religion* in the end an unsatisfactory work is not Kant's introduction of religious concepts into morality, but his humanistic faith in the unbounded power of pure reason, both to disclose the truth about man's moral situation, and to overcome innate evil in its own power. It is clearer to those who stand in a different culture and age from Kant how much his basic view of ethics derives, not from a supposed eternal reason, but from a rather over-zealous Pietistic, and certainly Christian, background.

9.3 THE NATURE OF RELIGIOUS SYMBOLS

In Book Two of the *Religion*, Kant develops a view of Christian doctrines as symbolic of the conflict of the good and evil principles which are expressed in man's freely chosen ultimate maxims. Thus the Devil symbolises the power of one's own evil choice; Heaven and Hell symbolise the radical gulf between the pure and impure will; the Holy Spirit becomes our confidence in our own moral disposition; and Christ symbolises that moral perfection which is the final end of creation. But such ideas 'reside in our morally-legislative reason'; their empirical instantiation, if any, is morally worthless. (Rel. 55; Ber. 6, 62.) Whether Jesus ever existed or not is beside the point; he is the 'archetype of the pure moral disposition', which all men must imitate in themselves. 'Only faith in the practical validity of the archetype has moral worth'; so belief in the divinity, or even historicity, of Jesus 'in no way benefits us practically'. Indeed, belief in his divinity might make us less sure of the attainability of the ideal by ourselves.

This view of religious concepts as pictures having practical, but no theoretical, force, is elaborated in an essay *On the End of All Things* (1794). Kant speaks of the concept of 'eternity' as sublime, dreadful yet fascinating: 'While we now follow up the transition from time to eternity . . . we encounter the end of all things . . . which, in the moral order of purposes, is simultaneously the beginning of a duration of these self-same beings as

supersensible . . . [which] will be susceptible of no other definition of its nature than a moral one'. (OH, 69 f.; Ber. 8, 327.) The
idea of an 'end of all things', a Last Day, originates solely from
reasoning about the moral course of the world; so 'the representation of those last things . . . must only be regarded as making
Doomsday . . . which is not theoretically conceivable to us, in
some way perceptible'. (OH, 71; Ber. 8, 328.)

Such pictures, of Heaven and Hell and Judgment Day, are not
theoretical dogmas, but have purely practical value, namely, that
we must act as if, in another life, the judgments of our own
conscience will be made absolute and unalterable. Doctrines of
the Apocalypse express man's awareness of his moral purpose and
his depravity and are effective in leading him to renewed moral
endeavour. So Kant suggests that the theory of universal salvation
should be rejected, because it may lessen the sense of the ultimate
significance of moral choice; though it may be preserved, in
another aspect, as expressing the triumph of God's love. Again,
we regard the future life as an endless moral progress, with a
changeless moral disposition to the good. However, such a picture
still presents 'simultaneously one prospect in an unending series
of evils', since each stage must be worse than its subsequent state.
(OH, 79; Ber. 8, 335.) And so man also thinks of the future life as
a static eternity, in which rest can at last be found, but at the cost
of absolute changelessness. Both contradictory pictures have
important practical functions; but clearly both cannot be true, as
conceived. Here reason reaches its ultimate limit, and is en-
tangled in contradictions; and this is a warning to it to keep to its
proper, practical, immanent use, rather than attempt to work out
the geography of the next world.

The limitations of speculative reason in the sphere of religion
are emphasised by Kant when he admits the existence of totally
incomprehensible 'holy mysteries' in religion. He defines a
mystery, rather inadequately, as something which may be
'known by each single individual but cannot be made known
publicly'. (Rel. 129; Ber. 6, 137.) He proceeds to explain that he
is thinking of those ideas which are known to practical reason,
and are necessary for practical use, but which are quite incomprehensible to speculative reason. The basic mystery, in this sense,
is that regarding what God may do to supplement our moral
inabilities, to bring about the *summum bonum*. This mystery can

be subdivided into three forms. First is the mystery of the Divine call to a moral end. 'The call to this end is morally quite clear' (Rel. 134; Ber. 6, 143); but for speculation the possibility of the creation of free moral agents is incomprehensible. It seems impossible for a being to be both a creature and yet totally free. In the second *Critique* Kant had tried to resolve this difficulty by suggesting that 'creation concerns intelligible but not sensuous existence'; so God is thought of as the creator of noumena, but not of appearances. (CPR, 106; Ber. 5, 103.) This putative solution is clearly unsatisfactory; and Kant now says that the problem is theoretically unresolvable, though from a practical point of view one must postulate both creation and freedom.

Second, is the mystery of atonement. Man as we know him is corrupt, and so he stands in need of Divine grace; 'But this contradicts spontaneity', according to which all moral good or evil must come from the individual himself. (Rel. 134; Ber. 6, 143.) So it is incomprehensible how 'out of evil good could spring up' (Rel. 134; Ber. 6, 143), or how God can bring men to realise the *summum bonum* when they have chosen evil. There is an antinomy here between the necessity for atonement before the evil disposition can be overcome, and the necessity that good works should precede faith, if one is to hope for atonement. This antinomy is theoretically undecidable; but in practice there can be no doubt that we must first become worthy of God's assistance through moral effort, and not begin with mere belief in what God has done for us. The doctrine of objective atonement is only necessary for making comprehensible the possibility of moral improvement. It does not enjoin faith in the historical man Jesus, but faith in the moral archetype which resides in reason itself; i.e. the moral principle itself. To have faith in the perfect man is to have faith in the moral archetype within; to have faith in moral improvement is to have faith in the same thing, under another aspect, that of the moral law. Thus the Divine forgiveness and moral striving are 'one and the same practical idea'; man's own moral commitment is at the same time and by the same act a sacrificial 'dying' to evil. Even so, forgiveness and fulfilment still seem impossible for men, since they never manage to commit themselves unreservedly to morality. And so the antinomy returns in its full force; the contradiction of grace and spontaneity must be accepted as the second mystery.

Third is 'the mystery of election'. Why some men should choose final good and others final evil, despite all the works of grace; and how God's purpose can coexist with the finally evil choices of some of his creatures, are again matters quite beyond human comprehension. Such questions utterly 'transcend all our concepts'.

The concepts which we adopt to render morality intelligible and by means of which we present moral ideas in sensible terms appear to be paradoxical and contradictory, when interpreted speculatively—i.e. as straightforward fact-stating claims. For example, God's love is represented by the picture of his self-sacrifice on the Cross. But we cannot infer that the intelligible reality is really in any way like the analogon we have needed to depict it. The analogy is only needed to make a concept intelligible to us; we cannot infer that it is a condition of the thing in itself. Indeed, we know that it cannot be, for an all-sufficient, changeless being cannot sacrifice himself in any real sense. So these religious pictures are not predicates giving even analogous knowledge of their object; their sole use is practical, to make moral concepts comprehensible to us.

It may seem that Kant regards religious symbols as translatable into moral concepts without remainder. But though it is true that they have purely practical force, it must be remembered that Kant is irrevocably committed to belief in a world beyond this one, in which moral purposes may triumph. And religious concepts must in some way symbolise that world, even though it is impossible for them to describe it, even analogically. Some clue as to their function in this respect is given by Kant's doctrine of 'aesthetic ideas', as he outlines it in the third *Critique*.

An aesthetic idea is a 'representation of the imagination . . . with which . . . such a multiplicity of partial representations are bound up, that no . . . definite concept can be found for it'. (CAJ, 179; Ber. 5, 316.) It is an intuition to which no concept can be adequate; such ideas 'strain after something lying out beyond the confines of experience', and so represent imaginatively pure rational concepts. (CAJ, 176; Ber. 5, 314.) Kant suggests that they express what is indefinable in a particular mental state in such a way that it can be communicated to others.

Religious symbols seem to share these characteristics of aesthetic ideas; and, indeed, to be generated, as aesthetic ideas are, by an innate endowment of unusual human beings, possessing the quality of genius. Thus they are not reducible to fact-stating assertions at all; one should not ask what they mean, taken literally. Their use is to determine the will to moral action; and what they symbolise, in a unique and untranslatable way, is the moral aspect of human experience and the intelligible reality which is the context of moral action.

So it is not satisfactory to interpret Kant as a complete reductionist in religious doctrine. Though his interpretation of Christian doctrine has the odd result of making almost all Christian devotional practices either superfluous or repugnant, nevertheless he holds 'that, through the moral law, man is called to a good course of life; that . . . he finds in himself justification for confidence in this good spirit and for hope that . . . he will be able to satisfy this spirit; finally, that . . . he must continually test himself as though summoned to account before a judge—reason, heart and conscience all teach this and urge its fulfilment'. (Rel. 135; Ber. 6, 144 f.)

These basic characteristics of absolute call; hope of fulfilment; continual, often losing warfare and faith in progress define a deeply religious view of ethics. They supply a note of intensity which is lacking in accounts of Kant which stress only the formalistic criteria of universalisability, autonomy and respect for persons as ends. Kant's own rationalism—his belief in one universal and absolute standard of reason, evident to all men—and his formalism—his belief that reason itself could promulgate all things necessary to the moral life—which led him to reject revealed religion in any form, are in tension with this fundamentally religious vision. To that extent his real view of ethics is never captured by his explicit accounts of that view.

9.4 THE EVOLUTION OF MORAL FAITH

In books three and four of the *Religion* Kant asserts that the good principle can only triumph over evil finally when an 'ethical commonwealth', a union of men under purely moral laws, comes into being—though, he says, 'we can never hope that man's good will will lead mankind to decide to work with unanimity towards this goal'. (Rel. 86; Ber. 6, 95.) This ideal is that of a 'people of God', wherein God is the one who gives the law and rewards his people in accordance with their inner dispositions. But while Kant holds that only God could found such a commonwealth, since men never will, yet 'must man proceed as though everything depended upon him'. (Rel. 92; Ber. 6, 100.) This ideal community should be 'a voluntary, universal and enduring union of hearts', a Moral Church. (Rel. 93; Ber. 6, 102.)

Kant holds that every ecclesiastical faith, which is founded in some historical revelation, is perhaps a means to bringing about the moral church; but such faiths must wither away, for claims to revelation are incompatible with universality. Moreover, no ecclesiastical faith can have any moral import—'historical faith ... contains nothing, and leads to nothing, which could have any moral value for us'; it must finally 'become mere faith in Scriptural scholars and their insight'. (Rel. 102, 105; Ber. 6, 111, 114.)

Ecclesiastical faith in fact precedes religious faith (in the moral life); and, for many people, remains its vehicle. So Kant is prepared to accept the Bible as revelation, as long as it is expounded according to morality and as long as men always seek to improve the church's form towards the one ideal moral community. But that coming of the Kingdom for which Christians look will in fact be the transition from their own form of particular ecclesiastical faith to the pure ethical commonwealth. If this comes about, the victory over evil will be won, and eternal peace will result.

Kant maintains that men have a special duty to join and obey the statutory rules of a visible church, since only the existence of such a church can enable the ethical commonwealth to develop out of revealed faiths. But on the other hand the church is by no means essential to the service of God in general. Kant is totally opposed to any devotional exercises to God, except as a means to cultivating the moral disposition; or to any characterisation of God in anthropomorphic terms, as a tyrant or ruler with an arbitrary will. Only problematic assumptions of God are required to enable us to strive to our moral goal; any claim to experience the presence of God is a superstitious illusion. Morality, in its relation to a final end, requires the postulation of God as legislator, benevolent ruler and righteous judge; but such a God cannot be an object of experience.

Further, it is not possible to recognise the working of grace in any human experience, still less actually produce grace by some activity such as prayer. Grace must only be postulated as the unknowable supplement to our moral insufficiencies; how or where it works is quite beyond our power to say. Religion adds hope of the consummation of the *summum bonum* to morality; and it may be said to comprise fear of God (respect for the law) and love of God (the liking to do duties as Divine commands). Our goal, then, is to love the law. But we can never completely attain this; and for finite creatures, respect must always be the primary attitude to it. (Cf. Rel. 136; Ber. 6, 145.) In this doctrine, Kant opposes that aspect of Pietistic religion which values the love which springs from faith above respect for morality. He regards love simply as the liking to do one's duty, which, though an ideal, cannot be attained by or be obligatory upon all men.

Love is certainly not, for Kant, any direct relationship with God: 'The feeling of the immediate presence of the Supreme Being' is 'the moral death of Reason', he writes (Rel. 163; Ber. 6, 175); no experience of supersensible beings is possible for man. So Kant will admit private prayer as a means of establishing goodness in oneself; church-going as the spreading abroad of moral effort; baptism as the reception into a moral community; and communion as a means for the maintenance of fellowship. But he rejects absolutely faith in miracles, sacramental mysteries and means of grace; any impetratory power of prayer; and any value in ritual acts of worship or pietistic reliance on grace, instead of moral endeavour.

Even if his ethics is fundamentally religious, it is not compatible with Christianity, in most of its forms. The divide appears because of his refusal to think of 'God' as in possible interaction with men, an object of experience and an agent able to influence states and human dispositions. 'God' is purely a postulate, a 'model' to render intelligible the general view of morality as a heroic warfare aimed at a necessary final end.

Thus conscience 'must be conceived as a subjective principle of responsibility before God.' (MM, 105; Ber. 6, 439.) We must posit the idea of an ideal judge and author of the law, who warns, prosecutes and has power to give the law its due effect. But we do not say that God really exists; the idea is an as-if postulate of regulative, subjective, practical reason, the use of which is to guide man to think of conscientiousness as responsibility before a holy being distinct from man yet present in his inmost being.

It follows, too, that 'there are no special duties to God . . . awe is . . . the religious temper in all our actions done in conformity with duty'. (Rel. 142; Ber. 6, 154.) 'The idea of God proceeds entirely from our own reason and *we ourselves make it.*' (MM, 110; Ber. 6, 443.) It is a duty to oneself, not to God, to apply this idea to the moral law. One cannot speak of God as though there could be moral relations between men and such an existing, personalised being: 'The sort of moral relation that holds . . . between God and man . . . is altogether inconceivable to us.' (MM, 167; Ber. 6, 491.) One could never render the concepts of duty and right, justice and benevolence, consistent as between God and men. So again the idea of God must be seen as self-created by reason, to make moral necessitation intelligible and strengthen one's motivations to morality. The formula which Kant uses most frequently in this respect is: 'Religion is . . . the recognition of all duties as divine commands.' (Rel. 142; Ber. 6, 153.) Religious belief must be grounded upon morality, and upon nothing else. In seeing duties as divine commands, it uses the theoretically problematic hypothesis that there is a highest intelligent cause of all things, as a model to make conceivable to man the realisation of the 'assertorial faith' that the ultimate aim of moral action can be realised.

This 'as-if' postulate of God arises, however, not only from consideration of how the *summum bonum* could be possible in the world, but also within moral experience itself. In the third *Critique*, Kant writes that, in beautiful surroundings, men feel 'a need of being grateful for it to someone'. (CTJ, 112; Ber. 5, 445.) Or, in a situation which calls for self-sacrifice, men feel a need of having 'carried out some command and obeyed a Supreme Lord'. (*Loc. cit.*) Again, after some moral default men 'seem to hear the voice of a judge' who reproaches them. Such feelings as these are natural and necessary to the man of moral feeling, and they are 'immediately connected with the purest moral sentiment', being 'special modes of a mental disposition towards duty'. (CTJ, 113; Ber. 5, 446.) Here, Kant is affirming, there is a 'pure moral need' for postulating the existence of a moral Intelligence, which has formed the world with a moral end in view. And in the cultivation of these feelings of gratitude, obedience and penitence, morality itself gains in strength.

Thus the idea of God, *qua* moral legislator, springs from 'the original moral bent of our nature, as a subjective principle'. (CTJ, 113; Ber. 5, 446.) We make the idea of God for use in moral experience itself as well as in the thought of the goal to which morality directs us. In both cases, the common root of the idea is a feeling of the insufficiency of the contingent for realising the 'moral destination of man's existence'. The imagined supposition of a supreme moral intelligence thus helps to regulate our attitudes in specific ways, as dictated by morality itself.

CHAPTER TEN

THE FINAL VIEW OF ETHICS

10.1 THE OPUS POSTUMUM

Kant's final conception of the relation of God and morality, and the fullest development of the metaphysical context of morality is to be found in the large collection of notes and jottings written down by Kant between about 1790–1803, which have been collected as the *Opus Postumum* (now in Ber. 21; 22). The central and fundamental place of the concept of God in Kant's view of ethics is made explicit in Sections 1 and 7, in particular, dated by Adickes as written between 1800–3.[1]

Adickes has claimed that the *Opus Postumum* shows a definite change in Kant's view of the relation of religion and morality. He claims that Kant, for some admittedly unknown reason, abandoned the doctrine of God as a postulate for correlating virtue with happiness, and proposed in its place a doctrine of complete immanentism, for which the concept of God becomes either a mere objectification of the moral law within, or the referent for a directly experienced personal being which makes itself felt immediately in the moral law. On the former interpretation the concept is an alternative, optional terminology for the moral law; while on the latter interpretation, the moral law is a vehicle of real experience of a personally conceived being. Either view would constitute a radical change in Kant's doctrine of the relation of morality and religion. For both imply the repudiation of the view that religious beliefs are conditions of the intelligibility of moral beliefs, but are not involved inherently in moral experience itself.

It is extremely difficult to evaluate such claims, which are made with reference to a large collection of manuscript jottings, set down often as more or less random or momentary thoughts,

[1] E. Adickes, *Kant's Opus Postumum* (von Reuther and Reichard, Berlin, 1920).

and often ending abruptly, even in mid sentence. Moreover, it is apparent that the notes are often in open contradiction with each other—thus Kant speaks of God as 'not a being outside me but merely a thought within me', and also as 'a being which is the absolute cause of the Universe'. (Ber. 21, 145. Ber. 21, 19.) One can deal with such difficulties in a number of ways—by supposing a development in thinking; or by supposing advancing senility; by interpreting such statements as really consistent, if more fully expressed; or by seeing them as dialectical steps in an argument in which Kant was his own Devil's advocate.

But the most reasonable approach would seem to be that one should, if possible, assume that Kant's Critical conclusions remained unchanged and try to interpret the obscure passages in terms of his earlier doctrines, unless there is some explicit repudiation of an earlier view. Adickes, who in general adheres to this principle, seems to abandon it when commenting on Kant's doctrine of God. For the only reasons he gives for asserting that Kant abandoned the 'moral argument' are that he did not restate it or comment upon it in the *Opus Postumum*; and that Kant states that no proof of God is possible. The latter statement is entirely consonant with Kant's Critical position, wherein he does not regard the moral argument as a theoretical proof. And the former shows, if anything, that Kant was quite satisfied with the formulations of the argument which he already had.

The question of immanentism is more complicated. Here at least there is positive textual evidence to be considered, though one must bear in mind Kant's lifelong opposition to any doctrine of a direct experience of God, and thus to the second interpretation of immanentism offered above. It will·be useful to cite the main strands of Kant's thinking about God in the *Opus Postumum*.

A number of passages suggest some form of subjectivist doctrine of God: 'To think the idea [of God] and to believe is an identical act'; 'God is not a thing subsisting outside me, but my own thought. It is absurd to ask whether a God exists.' (Ber. 22, 109. Ber. 21, 153.) In interpreting such passages, one must remember Kant's technical use of 'idea', as a necessary postulate of reason which, in the case of God, is given as a necessary condition of the possibility of the *summum bonum*, and so of an intelligible absolute morality.

There are frequent denials that God is an external substance:

'God is not a substance'; 'God must be represented not as substance outside me, but as the highest moral principle in me.' (Ber. 22, 108. Ber. 21, 144.) Again, this is equivalent to the denial that the existence of God can be theoretically established. One should not ask, 'Does God exist?', if that question leads one to undertake empirical researches or to indulge in speculative metaphysics. Rather, 'The proposition: there is a God, says nothing more than: there is in the human, morally self-determining reason a highest principle which determines itself, and finds itself compelled unremittingly to act in accordance with such a principle.' (Ber. 21, 146.) Or, more briefly, 'God is the morally practical self-legislative reason.' (Ber. 21, 145.)

The question is whether these passages identify God with the moral law within; or whether they rather suggest that the moral imperative directly reveals God (who would be an ontologically distinct being); or whether they are not quite consonant with the view that no direct experience of God is possible in any form, though duties can be seen as divine commands when the concept of God is postulated. Of these three alternatives, it seems to me that the second can be immediately dispensed with. In addition to Kant's insistence that direct revelation of God is metaphysically impossible and morally dangerous, the view would require a doctrine of God as a distinct existent who could reveal himself in moral experience. If anything at all is rejected by the quotations cited above, it is that it makes sense to speak of an externally existing being which is then revealed in certain experiences.

If the first view is taken to entail, not only that there is no 'external reality' *corresponding to* our idea of God, but also that there is no external reality in question at all, in speaking of God, the dispute in interpretation resolves itself into the more general dispute as to the status of noumena in the *Opus Postumum*. Here one must note the emphasis, to be found throughout the notes, on 'creative self-determination'. As Kant says, 'We make everything ourselves'; 'Space and time are products . . . of our own faculty of imagination'; 'Space and time are not things which exist outside the representation . . . they are that which the faculty of representation makes for itself.' (Ber. 22, 82. Ber. 22, 37. Ber. 22, 71.) There is an emphatic stress on the world as being self-posited, or a means of determining one's own being by intelligible creative action; and this goes with the elaboration of a theory in which even the particular laws of physics, the number of senses and other details of the empirical world can be deduced by pure rational considerations from the architectonic of pure reason. Kant is thus greatly extending the sphere of the rational, in the *Opus Postumum*; and he emphasises even more the creative role of reason in constituting its own being through rational action. The transition to a Hegelian type of idealism is clearly foreshadowed here, however much Kant declared his opposition to the Fichtean idealism which was making that transition in its own way.

It is with this in mind that one should read Kant's statement that God is 'the product of our own reason'. (Ber. 22, 117.) We make God only in the sense that we make every rational structure in the world; and such 'making' is necessary to a rational being. Indeed, a being constitutes itself as rational by making such an intelligible world. It would be inconsistent for such a view to deny altogether the existence of a non-phenomenal reality. For it is not that intelligible realities are 'as-if' fictions on the edge of a stable empirical reality. Rather, empirical reality only exists within the transcendental structures of active reason, the ways in which rational beings creatively 'posit' themselves; and the ground of all this 'making' is most decidedly not empirical.

Whereas in the first *Critique* one might suspect that Kant wished to identify the 'noumenal ground' with the rational self, he openly suggests now that the self, too, is determined by the activity of creative self-positing—i.e. the source of rational activity is beyond one's personal, individual self; so that he can hold even more firmly that nothing can be said of such a source. In one place Kant writes, 'I make myself.' (Ber. 22, 82.) It seems clear, from many such passages, that Kant retains the doctrine of noumena, and indeed moves towards a doctrine in which the whole world, including the subject-object dichotomy, becomes a creative self-positing of reason itself.

The concept of 'God', as a purely rational concept, plays its part in this scheme as an idea of reason, a postulate of morally-practical reason. So, whereas Kant certainly says that God is self-legislative reason, he does not mean that it is a pure fiction; though it is senseless to ask what, in reality, corresponds to it. It is not a fiction, because even to think of it in such terms is to think of it as 'possibly, but not in fact, real'; or as merely a figment of the imagination; whereas it could not possibly be empirically real, and it is a necessary idea of reason. The whole point of Kant's argument is that one should come to recognise that the dichotomy 'real/fictional' simply cannot apply to the concept of 'God'. The concept is necessary but practical. It is bound up with a specific sort of moral commitment. One should not press illegitimate questions upon it.

Thus to identify God with 'practical reason in me', or to assert that 'God is not a substance', is not to deny that the concept has any objective validity; and it is certainly not to say that God is immanent, in the sense of being some psychological force. It is to identify God with the unknowable, unitary, self-positing source of the rational structures of reality; and, in particular, with this source as it is expressed in the morally practical reason of the individual rational agent.

10.2 GOD AND PRACTICAL REASON

There is a development in the *Opus Postumum* from the Critical doctrine that 'God' is a postulate which can have no direct influence on the moral life, an unknown, unexperiencable somewhat which makes the *summum bonum* possible. For in the *Opus Postumum*, Kant makes explicit a doctrine which is implicit in many earlier works, that God and practical reason are identical.

The view is clearly expressed thus: 'There is a Being in me, distinguished from myself as the cause of an effect wrought upon me, which freely . . . judges me within, justifying or condemning me; and I as man am myself this being, and it is no substance external to me, and . . . its causality is no natural necessity but a determination of me to a free act'. (Ber. 21, 25.) Here Kant distinguishes *wille* (practical reason) and *willkur* (the faculty of choice); the 'being in me' which is also 'myself, as man', not an external substance, and the 'faculty of choice', which is judged by my superior self. The true man and the true self are thus identical with God and truly free; practical reason is somehow one in all men, the unitary intelligible ground of nature itself. Yet, *qua willkur*, man is subject to sensuous as well as rational motives and impulses, and he in fact has everywhere freely subjected himself to heteronomous determination by nature.

Thus though the moral law is the law of man's own nature, immanent in him and promulgated by him; nevertheless it is not the law his will (*willkur*) has freely adopted into the maxims of his willing. Man has somehow been able to alienate himself from his 'true self', by a free decision of will, which renders him incapable of fulfilling the demands of his own nature, and nature incapable of providing the final good for man. Man is in radical evil, in thrall to the powers of sensuous nature, alienated from the ground of his own humanity. The best one can do, in face of the absolute demand of the immanent God, and one's free alienation from it, is to hope for reconciliation by the pursuit of virtue through moral struggle for eternity. This prospect is a rather depressing and insecure one; but the central notions of demand, alienation and reconciliation elaborate further Kant's essentially religious view of ethics.

The identification of God and practical reason, made repeatedly throughout the *Opus Postumum*, is not explicitly stated in any prior works, though it does make clearer many of Kant's previous doctrines, such as his teaching on atonement, in the *Religion* (cf. 9.3), and his notion that the noumenal self must be conceived as determining phenomenal nature, in the second *Critique* (cf. 6.3). So one must assume that while Kant retained the 'moral argument', with its concept of 'God' as a condition of the possibility of the moral end, he also modified the notion of 'God' in the *Opus Postumum* so that God not only makes nature able to accommodate the *summum bonum*, but also directly promulgates the moral law, enacts it in one and judges one's performance. And, in all this, there is a sense in which God is identical both with my real, or rational, self, and with the selves of all rational men.

This doctrine, the last we have from Kant's pen, is the final consequence of his insistence upon autonomy, the self-legislation of morality. 'In the world [he writes] there is a totality of morally-practical reason, and consequently of an imperative Right, and therewith also a God.' (Ber. 21, 11.) It does not seem to be true, as Adickes has suggested, that Kant now finds, in the consciousness of the moral law itself, a consciousness of being in the presence of a personal God, or that he founds theistic belief on immediate subjective personal experience. Though Kant speaks of God as Personality for the first time in the *Opus Postumum*, he means by 'Personality' simply the legislative capacity of originative reason, and not the sort of subjectivity that belongs to human persons. God *is* reason, or the 'imperative Right', and is known in the categorical imperative; but this God is also man's true intelligible self. The doctrine is expressed clearly thus: 'The conception of God is . . . the pure practical reason itself in its Personality and with executive powers in relation to the system of the world and its forces.' (Ber. 22, 118.) God is a Personality, not external to man as a separate substance, but within man. Nevertheless, this God has 'executive power' over nature—which is a clear expression of the 'moral argument' for postulating a Divine moral ordering of nature, which can ensure that the absolute moral demands can finally be fully met.

10.3 THE METAPHYSICAL CONTEXT OF KANT'S ETHICS

Kant never attained a clear, consistent and complete doctrine of the metaphysical context of ethics. These comments in the *Opus Postumum*, though they illuminate much of what Kant had previously written, leave a plethora of obscurities about the relation of God and man, practical reason and free will, reason and nature. But it should be quite plain that the ethical writings after the *Groundwork* are not just addenda to an essentially complete system of ethics. They are expressions of Kant's continually renewed attempts to find a satisfactory conceptual framework for the view of morality which underlay the *Groundwork* formulation of the categorical imperative. I have attempted to trace the development of this view through the corpus of Kant's works, and to show that it is one recognisably identical view, even though it is a developing one. And I have tried to show how the parallel development in Kant's metaphysical thinking both enabled him to offer an intelligible account of morality, and yet, at the same time, left him with a terminology which was quite unsuited to express his view consistently.

Kant's view of ethics ends, in the *Religion* and the *Opus Postumum*, in a tangle of contradictions and antinomies, in which Kant is constantly saying what is on his own terms unsayable, and saying it in contradictory ways. His excuse is that he has here passed beyond the limits of reason; but it seems more likely that he has passed beyond the limits of the Critical philosophy, but is unable to accept the fact. I wish to suggest that Kant's final view is not *just* a set of contradictions, but that it not only expresses a view of the nature of ethics without which such works as the *Groundwork* remain largely unintelligible; but also that it reveals the inadequacy of the doctrines of the Critical philosophy to express this view coherently. Many, if not most, of the common misunderstandings of Kant's ethics derive from ignorance of this wider context of the categorical imperative. I have tried, not to support or argue in favour of Kant's view, but simply to make the wider context clear, and thus prepare the way for a more adequate understanding of Kant's view of ethics.

The basic problem is that Kant has left a deeply religious ethics expressed in a radically humanistic terminology. He propounds a view of man as involved in an impersonal but purposive nature; as inevitably faced with endless struggle and suffering in an attempt to gain virtue; as part of an evolutionary process moving towards a universal world-society, yet as born for an eternal destiny of moral progress beyond this space-time world. Kant sees moral freedom and struggle as of supreme value; without it happiness is no more than an animal contentment without point. But such struggle entails estrangement in nature, a realm with its own laws and purposes; a realm which does provide hints of a higher moral purpose, but is unable to provide such a purpose. And, though man is innately evil, by virtue of his estrangement in the world, yet his true rational self remains identical with the God which is the ground of both nature and humanity. So he may hope for an ultimate destiny in which reason and nature are reconciled in some unknown way. He may even hope for Divine help in attaining that end, though again he cannot know how it will come.

The general scheme is unmistakably Christian in origin; but it significantly amends Christian doctrine in a number of ways. The universe is a purposive creation of God; but it is also the self-expressive appearance of the being of God, who is himself present, *qua* practical reason, in all men. There is a 'Fall' into original sin; but this is a fall which is virtually inevitable in view of man's search for self-sufficiency and moral responsibility. There is a consummation at the last day to be hoped for; but it is more the hope of happiness in the attainment of perfection through the pursuit of virtue than a redemption purchased

M*

through Divine sacrifice. In a sense one may say that human history is itself the Divine sacrifice, since it is the incarnation of practical reason in phenomenal nature. So far Kant's view seems not radically unlike the traditional Christian view. But any sense of personal fellowship with God, revelation from God or redemption by God is entirely lacking in the Kantian scheme.

I think one must conclude that the view is unsatisfactory and incomplete, as it stands. It has abandoned the orthodox Christian stress on the independence of the individual in relation to God; but it does not embrace the later Hegelian view of the space-time world as the temporal manifestation of one absolutely rational reality, for which individuals are subordinate parts. Thus there remains in Kant to the end that tension of freedom and rational intelligibility, Wolffian rationalism and individualistic Pietism, from which he started.

10.4 THE CONFLICT OF RATIONALISM AND INDIVIDUALISM

There are a number of strands in Kant's thought which do not easily hold together, but which all help to define his view in some way.

One strand is his rationalism, which leads him to emphasise the intelligible structure of the whole rather than the unpredictable uniqueness of particular individuals and which prevents him from accepting any doctrine of revelation or grace, even though his own interpretation of the Fall seems to require such a doctrine.

Another strand, in marked tension with this, is his individualism, which leads him to set a supreme worth on individual moral struggle and to leave human freedom as a non-rational, intelligibly incomprehensible fact, on which the destiny of the human race yet depends. The supreme importance which he attributes to the sheer contingency of human life, in its moral endeavours, is hard to reconcile with his vision of the universe as a completely intelligible, unitary whole. The tension comes to a head in the doctrine of autonomy, where Kant speaks in radically humanistic terms of the freedom of human choice in its total self-determination; and yet he identifies practical reason with God, as perfectly rational in its action and as one in all men. It always remains unclear whether freedom is a finally non-rational property of human individuals or simply the action of God, *qua* practical reason, in men, working unhampered by nature.

Thus Kant holds that 'Freedom and self-legislation of the will . . . are reciprocal conceptions.' (G, 83; Ber. 4, 450.) Also, 'Freedom of choice is this independence from sensuous impulse in the determination of choice. This is the negative concept of freedom. The positive concept of freedom is that of the power of pure reason to be of itself practical.' (MM, 10; Ber. 6, 213 f.) 'The possibility of deviating from legislative reason is a lack of power. How, then, can this possibility be used to define freedom?' (MM, 26; Ber. 6, 227.)

Kant seems to imply in these passages that a man is only free when he is rationally determined, and vice versa. And this line of thought is reflected in his comments that reason itself 'produces' reverence for the law, that it legislates the moral law, and, *qua* practical reason, actually determines action in accordance with law. But this account of freedom excludes just that notion of 'moral obligation' which Kant wishes to explain, the notion of being constrained but not compelled, even by reason, to do something. And it leaves totally obscure the place of the 'faculty of choice'—*willkur*—in the moral life. If freedom is rational determination, it becomes quite inexplicable that man, as a sensuous being with desires, should be free either to implement the moral law or to be governed by desires. To allow desires to overcome the dictates of practical reason is simply 'lack of power', a sort of failure of reason as an efficient cause.

This is a Lutheran picture of human nature as controlled by one of two forces, reason or desire, but as not consciously choosing which one is in control. Man is a sort of battleground of these two impersonal forces, a passive spectator of the war between reason and desire which plays itself out in his own being.

One difficulty with this picture is that, whereas reason represents noumenal spontaneity, the desires are purely phenomenal, mere appearances of an unknown noumenal reality. But how can reality enter into a conflict with appearances? And what, in noumenal reality, do the desires express? It seems that, if the battle is real, it must be between intelligible forces; but what sort of internal conflict could it be? Nature must at once express rational reality—simply because it is 'appearance'—but at the same time be a recalcitrant force, capable of perverting or overpowering reason. And in this recalcitrant function it must be the proving-ground on which reason is able to assert its dominance and shape nature to its own ends, not by negating but by fulfilling it. The place of sensuous nature in the overall pattern of intelligible reality needs to be more precisely determined.

The other main difficulty with the picture is that man himself has the final, ineluctable responsibility both for moral failure and moral success. Thus he cannot be purely passive in this struggle, after all, but must enter actively into it. 'What is it in you that can be trusted to enter into combat with all the powers of nature in you and around you and, if they come into conflict with your moral principles, to conquer them?', asks Kant rhetorically. (MM, 157; Ber. 6, 483.) Practical reason can fulfil and transcend nature, but it is the individual himself who bears responsibility for this task. As a human being, man 'can never be wholly free from desires . . . which . . . do not of themselves agree with the moral law'; and so 'the moral condition which he can always be in is virtue, i.e. moral disposition in conflict, and not holiness'. (CPR, 86; Ber. 5, 84. CPR, 87; Ber. 5, 84.) All the worth of human life lies, not in happiness, but in the cultivation of the good will and the consciousness of one's ultimate freedom over nature, which is realised in the continuance of moral struggle.

This stress on individual freedom and struggle is not easy to reconcile with the general picture of a 'universal practical reason', necessarily acting according to purely rational laws. And the tension pin-points one central problem of Kant's ethical theory, the problem of how the self which is free to accept or reject the moral law can somehow be the same self which necessarily promulgates that law. Kant speaks of *wille*, practical reason, as being the 'true self'; and yet it is *willkur*, the faculty of choice embodied in a sensuous human being, which must attain moral worth through struggle and moral effort. *Willkur* must freely decide to obey *wille*; and it is this free obedience which is of absolute worth. The arbitrary freedom of *willkur* is not of absolute worth in itself; but neither is automatic action in accordance with *wille* (though Kant suggests that it is). What is of worth is action from the motive of obedience to *wille*; and freedom is the condition of such action. However, the plain fact is that if I can freely obey or disobey *wille*, and if it does command my imperfectly rational *willkur*, then *wille* is as heteronomous as any objective moral value. Kant's proposal that moral cognitions can be action-guiding (that reason can be morally practical) because I myself promulgate the moral law, collapses when the 'I' is seen to be radically ambiguous between *wille*, which promulgates the law, and *willkur*, which is free to obey or disobey it. The irony is that Kant believes that morality entails freedom; but he construes freedom as rational determination, and holds that this 'explains' the fact of obligation. But the freedom which is entailed by morality precludes any possibility of explanation— there can, in principle, be no answer to the question, 'Why choose to obey or disobey reason?'. This is the inexplicable freedom of *willkur*. And the sort of determination by reason which Kant proposes as the essence of true freedom in fact excludes the notion of 'obligation', by reducing it to a quasi-causal determination, following principles to which a fully rational being is necessarily bound. This is the necessarily determined freedom of *wille*. Kant never resolves this incoherence in his concept of freedom. Much more needs to be said about reason (*wille*) and its relation to the faculty of choice (*willkur*) to make sense of the Kantian picture of the moral life as a struggle to attain virtue, a struggle which may, presumably, be lost as well as won.

10.5 KANT'S VOLUNTARISM

The third main strand in Kant's view of ethics is what Richard Kroner has called Kant's 'voluntarism'—his rejection of all speculative accounts of the nature of reality in favour of commitment to moral willing, and a rejection of all material ends of action in favour of purely formal criteria of action—what I have referred to as his 'formalism'. In both these aspects, Kant is rejecting the speculative intellect and any form of intuition as a basis for ethics, and proposing to find that basis in the activity of the will itself, acting according to purely rational criteria.

He thus rejects empiricism, which 'uproots the morality of intentions'; and mysticism, which deduces the nature of virtuous action from the intellectual contemplation of 'perfection'. Morality entails the falsity of empiricism; but it is also the case that ignorance of God and one's eternal destiny is necessary for the moral life, as is lack of determination by any material ends of action, which, he holds, would all be empirical and contingent.

Kant considers that self-interest would inevitably enter in, if such knowledge was possible. Moral action must be completely self-determining; although it necessarily involves belief in God and immortality and commitment to specific ends of action, knowledge of these cannot precede the moral law without undermining it. It follows that as long as morality remains, speculative ignorance must remain; in this sense, as Kroner says, 'morality makes the world incomprehensible'.[2] As long as man is bound by absolute obligations and remains morally free he must remain, at least to some extent, ignorant of God and his own future destiny. But here again the ultimate importance Kant wishes to attach to moral decision (which is Pietistic in origin) is in conflict with the Rationalist quest for intelligibility. It looks as though man is either eternally condemned to ignorance, or—when he attains full knowledge—must cease to be morally free and therefore truly individual. A possible solution to the conflict might be to make moral freedom and individuality a transitional and necessary stage in the self-expressive temporal appearance of intelligible reality. But it is highly doubtful that Kant would have accepted this solution; for such a view is still in conflict with a radical stress on the ultimate importance of moral obligation and individual freedom, which seems to be central to Kant's thinking.

In trying to replace speculative rationalism by a voluntaristic rationalism, Kant attempts to find a *via media* between the rationalism of Wolff and the stress on individual moral freedom of Pietism. He retains the rationalist criteria of unity, harmony, coherence and consistency; but he applies them to the will, *qua* practical reason, rather than to reason as a contemplative, intellectual faculty. But the reconciling gesture fails. The element of voluntarism makes the world incomprehensible and unknowable, undermining the possibility of rationalism; while the element of rationalism makes human freedom illusory and moral struggle inexplicable, undermining Pietistic individualism. So Kant, wishing somehow to defend both moral freedom and rational intelligibility, ends by losing both.

Moreover, the programme of voluntarism—that a completely formal principle should give rise to material ends of action and that a purely moral principle should entail factual assertions

[2] R. Kroner, *Kant's Weltanschauung*, trans. J. Smith (University of Chicago Press, 1956), p. 29.

about God and immortality—seems impossible in principle. I have shown how Kant implicitly relied on a Natural Law doctrine of substantive ends of nature, in order to derive ends of action from his formal principle. And it is also clear that his account of the nature of morality is only intelligible within the context of a specific metaphysical view which was constant throughout his life.

In its fully developed form, this is the view of one universal reason manifesting itself in empirical reality; somehow rendered ineffective in the actual conduct of men, so that they are involved in constant moral struggle, ignorance and failure; yet holding out the hope of a reunion of appearance and reality, of empirical happiness in the attainment of human perfection through the successful pursuit of virtue. It is only within such a metaphysical context of demand, alienation and reconciliation that the doctrine of the categorical imperative emerges in its true complexity.

Kant regards this view of morality as somehow 'given' in moral experience itself, which is experience of an absolute necessary claim and seemingly innate moral inability. So he holds that moral commitment must precede belief in God and in a future life, and that moral experience would be pathological if its practical postulates could be shown to be false. It seems clear, however, that Kant *is* giving a speculative account of reality, but one based on moral experience as opposed to reflection on the order or contingency of the physical world. As reason can come to know the categories which are involved in knowledge of physical reality, so it can come to know the formal characteristics involved in moral action—namely, the characteristics of a will acting according to universal, self-legislated law. In both cases, the account of reason promulgating formal principles, a common source of spontaneity in all men, is highly speculative, and is meant to justify the occurrence of synthetic *a priori* knowledge in physics and morals, respectively.

I have held that this view of morality itself arose out of Kant's early and continuing interest in a spiritual account of the nature and destiny of man; and that the formalistic vocabulary derived from the Critical philosophy is not well suited to express the central place which the postulates must take in Kant's ethics, or the centrality of his concern with the ends of moral action and the fulfilment of human personality. Moreover, it may seem to give a misleadingly humanistic tone to Kant's ethics, and serve to obscure the contradiction between rationalism and individualism, in talking of the autonomy and self-legislation of the reason of the individual.

But that contradiction, between, on the one hand, freedom and individualism; and on the other, organic unity and rationality, remains at the heart of Kant's view of ethics. The individualistic strain derives from the Pietistic emphasis on the unique importance of the individual and the final importance of his moral choices. But because of Kant's aversion to the notions of grace and personal fellowship with God, it often reads like a form of radical humanism. The rationalistic strain derives from the Wolff-Leibniz tradition in philosophy; but, though Kant tries to give it a purely formalistic and voluntaristic interpretation, he is never able to provide an intelligible account of the relation between practical reason and the freedom of choice of the human, not wholly rational, individual.

Kant's view of ethics is thus religious in origin and articulation. Virtue is seen as an intrinsically worthwhile struggle aimed at perfection, which brings self-wrought happiness in its attainment. Man is seen as absolutely obligated, morally incapable, yet called to hope for fulfilment. Kant's ultimate concern in ethics, it seems clear, was with human fulfilment in a harmonious and constantly developing community; his religious doctrines are attempts to establish the possibility of such fulfilment, which seems so uncertain in this life. But all this is expressed in a terminology which both conceals an inherent instability in the view and obscures its true character.

My aim, in presenting this exposition of the developing relation between Kant's ethical and metaphysical views, has been to explain the genesis of and to penetrate behind the terminology in which the ethical theory is expressed; to expound the underlying view so as to clarify and eliminate prevalent misunderstandings of Kant; and finally to expose a central contradiction within the view itself, which played a formative and creative part in the development of the view, and which remains an unsolved, perhaps unsolvable, metaphysical problem in Kant's thought on ethics.

SCHILPP'S
KANT'S PRE-CRITICAL ETHICS

In section 1.1, I stated that Paul Schilpp's interpretation of Kant's pre-Critical ethics was idiosyncratic. Since Schilpp's work is widely accepted as the standard text in English on the pre-Critical ethics and since it has been given a seal of approval by H. J. Paton, who contributed a foreword to the second edition, it is incumbent upon me to state briefly my objections to it.

The major respect in which Schilpp's interpretation differs from the one I have offered is that he denies that Kant ever took 'feeling' to be the ground of moral conduct. So, naturally, he denies that the British moral sense theorists were an important influence on the development of Kant's views, and he attempts to trace, in Kant's early writings, the development of a consistently rationalist view. The positive view he attributes to Kant, however, is a combination of pragmatism and process-philosophy, neither of which seems compatible with Kant's metaphysical theories. So while there is much valuable material in Schilpp's book, the thesis he attempts to support is so improbable that his interpretative comments on particular passages are often strained or even unintelligible.

His view is that Kant did not regard 'the formal' as a 'mould', to which material elements had to conform, but as a 'method' governing rational reflection. This method is to be taken in a temporal sense, and involves (1) rational reflection on the empirical data of human life; (2) the creation of new goals of moral endeavour; and (3) the transition from 'congenial old goods', or accepted objectives, to new, exploratory objectives (cf. S, 173). Morality is thus seen as a temporal process of the construction of new purposes by rational reflection and reciprocal response to other persons and changing situations. The 'method' is a method of temporal transition from accepted goals to new ones, more satisfying in prospect; and this, says Schilpp, is what Kant (admittedly not always consistently) meant by 'the formal' in morality.

Accordingly, he writes that Kant sees that 'the solution of an ethical problem involves a temporal transition to a new engrossment discontinuous with the present one which has been called in question'. (S, 130 f.) Teale, perhaps influenced by Schilpp, interprets the pre-Critical works in a similar way, holding that it was Kant's exploration of aesthetic judgment which led him to a view of morality as a creative, pragmatic, temporally developing process. So he, too, writes, 'Judgment . . . progressively frames rules for itself in order to guide and discipline its procedure . . . in the light of successes actually achieved'.[1] Both these interpretations show a remarkably unhistorical attitude.

Whenever Kant speaks of the 'creative function' of reason, Schilpp interprets this in a temporal sense, as a sort of dynamic evolution in time to new objectives, which it constructs imaginatively. He is right, of course, in his claim that the formal principle upon which Kant relies, in his developed Critical theory, is not that of bare self-contradiction, but is a much more teleological principle of the development of one's natural capacities for realising many sorts of purposes. But one should not confuse the statement that a formal principle decrees the development (no doubt temporal) of one's powers with the statement that the principle decrees a temporal development in one's conception of what the substantial ends of moral endeavour are. Kant's formal principle does not govern a change in the *ends* of moral action. In the case of perfect duties, there is no room for creative spontaneity at all; certain classes of action are absolutely prohibited. And in the case of imperfect duties, the ends of moral action are fixed necessarily and absolutely, once for all by the moral law (the ends, namely, of culture and beneficence). Any creative change must be in one's striving towards those ends, or in one's choice of particular acts which will realise them. The notion of 'spontaneity' must always be limited by the notion of the necessity of reason and its laws. The human person is spontaneous in being free from empirical determination; but he is not free from the necessary and unchanging principles according to which all

[1] A. E. Teale, *Kantian Ethics* (Oxford University Press, 1951), pp. 76 f.

rational beings must act. Reason, in both its theoretical and practical aspects, is logically rather than temporally spontaneous, for Kant, in that it legislates unchanging principles governing apprehension and action. These principles, and the essential ends of humanity, which they determine, are necessary, and so not subject to change or development.

In Kant's moral thinking there was never any doubt at all of the stringency of universal and necessary moral laws. So it is questionable to attribute to Kant, as Schilpp does, an interpretation of 'formal' which is inconsistent with Kant's own first-order moral beliefs. Such an interpretation permeates all Schilpp's commentary, and accounts for many of the obscure parts of his otherwise valuable exposition, especially his comments on the *Dreams* and the *Inaugural Dissertation*. It is by the use of such a pragmatist interpretation that Schilpp attempts to explain away the passages I have cited in the text which point to the influence of moral sense theories (cf. 2.2–4). If that interpretation is discarded—as I think it must be—the texts can be construed more straightforwardly on the lines I have suggested.

SELECT BIBLIOGRAPHY

ADICKES, E. *Kant's Opus Postumum* (von Reuther and Reichard, Berlin, 1920).

BECK, L. W. *A Commentary on Kant's Critique of Practical Reason* (University of Chicago Press, 1960).

DOWNIE, R. S. and TELFER E. *Respect for Persons* (Allen and Unwin, London, 1969).

DUNCAN, A. R. C. *Practical Reason and Morality* (Nelson, London, 1957).

ENGLAND, F. E. *Kant's Conception of God* (Allen and Unwin, London, 1929).

GREGOR, MARY J. *Laws of Freedom* (Blackwell, Oxford, 1963).

HARE, R. M. *The Language of Morals* (Oxford University Press, 1952).

JONES, W. T. *Morality and Freedom in the Philosophy of Kant* (Oxford University Press, 1940).

KEMP-SMITH, N. *A Commentary to Kant's 'Critique of Pure Reason'* (Macmillan, London, 1930).

KRONER, R. *Kant's Weltanschauung* trans. J. Smith (University of Chicago Press, 1956).

MENZER, B. P. 'Entwicklungsgang der Kantischen Ethik in den Jahren 1760–1785'; in *Kant-Studien* 2 (1898) and 3 (1899).

MURPHY, J. G. *Kant: The Philosophy of Right* (Macmillan, London, 1970).

PATON, H. J. *The Categorical Imperative* (Hutchinson's University Library, London, 1947).

PATON, H. J. *Kant's Metaphysic of Experience* (Allen and Unwin, London, 1936).

ROSS, W. D. *Kant's Ethical Theory: A Commentary on the 'Grundlegung zur Metaphysik der Sitten'* (Oxford University Press, 1954).

SCHILPP   P. A. *Kant's Pre-Critical Ethics* (Northwestern University Press, Evanston, 1960).

SCHRADER   G. 'Kant's Presumed Repudiation of the "Moral Argument" in the *Opus Postumum*'; in *Philosophy*, vol. 26; 1951).

SINGER, M. G. *Generalisation in Ethics* (Knopf, New York, 1961).

STRAWSON, P. F. *The Bounds of Sense* (Methuen, London, 1966).

STUCKENBERG, J. H. W. *Life of Immanuel Kant* (Macmillan, London, 1882).

TEALE, A. E. *Kantian Ethics* (Oxford University Press, 1951).

DE VLEESCHAUWER. *The Development of Kantian Thought* trans. A. R. Duncan (Nelson, Edinburgh, 1962).

WEBB, C. J. *Kant's Philosophy of Religion* (Oxford University Press, 1926).

WILLIAMS, T. C. *The Concept of the Categorical Imperative* (Oxford University Press, 1968).

WOOD, A. W. *Kant's Moral Religion* (Cornell University Press, Ithaca, 1970).

INDEX OF PERSONS

INDEX OF SUBJECTS

Major topics are listed in the Analytical Table of Contents.

Lightning Source UK Ltd.
Milton Keynes UK
UKHW022215200619
344768UK00008B/31/P